PRESENTED TO:

_____

PRESENTED BY:

_____

DATE:

_____

Every moment of this strange and lovely life
from dawn to dusk is a miracle.
Somewhere, always, a rose is opening its petals to the dawn.
Somewhere, always, a flower is fading in the dusk.

BEVERLY NICHOLS

101 THINGS
YOU SHOULD
DO BEFORE
GOING TO
HEAVEN

DAVID BORDON AND TOM WINTERS

WARNER
Faith®

New York Boston Nashville

Warner Faith

Time Warner Book Group
1271 Avenue of the Americas, New York, NY 10020
Visit our Web site at www.twbookmark.com

Warner Faith® and the Warner Faith logo are trademarks of Time Warner Book Group Inc.

Printed in the United States of America

First Edition: March 2006
10 9 8 7 6 5 4 3 2 1

ISBN: 0-446-57899-1

LLCN: 2005934581

Introduction

If you are a Christian, you can look forward to a magnificent eternity in heaven and your arrival there will be an indescribable homecoming. A new beginning. A new body. A new intimacy with God. A new life—one without end. No more pain. No more tears. No more sun or moon, because God's own glory will provide enough light. Although God hasn't provided you with a crystal-clear picture of what your eternal home will be like, you can be sure it will exceed your wildest dreams. It will be what your heart has always longed for here on earth but could never quite touch. It will be paradise in every sense of the word. But you're not there yet.

You may take the journey home tonight, tomorrow, or years down the road. This book you hold in your hands, *101 Things You Should Do Before Going to Heaven*, was written to help you prepare for your arrival in heaven by making the most of every day God has set aside for you here on earth. Take hold of the wonderful adventure God has planned for your life. And if you have not yet done so, take hold of His grace, forgiveness, and unfailing love. Then go out there and really live. There's a wild and wonderful world that's longing to catch a glimpse of God—and heaven—through you.

CONTENTS

A single event can awaken within us
a stranger totally unknown to us.
To live is to be slowly born.

ANTOINE DE SAINT-EXUPÉRY

101 THINGS
YOU SHOULD
DO BEFORE
GOING TO
HEAVEN

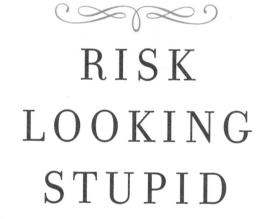

1

RISK
LOOKING
STUPID

Noah built a boat in his front yard before anyone knew what a "flood" really was. Moses "freed" the people of Israel by leading them to the edge of the impassable Red Sea. David—a boy with some rocks and a slingshot—volunteered to fight Goliath—a supersized warrior. Joshua told his troops they would defeat Jericho by marching around the city walls for six days while blowing horns. Jesus put some mud on the eyes of a blind man and proclaimed that the man could see. There had to have been some snickers. The murmur of skeptics. A few whispers among the crowd that voiced what others were thinking—"This is a really stupid idea!"

If you want to become the person God designed you to be, you need to risk looking stupid every once in a while. Those in the Bible who did exactly that accomplished some amazing things. But they also picked up a lot of criticism, and even a few enemies, along the way. That's because going against the grain of accepted wisdom and public opinion—even when you believe God is leading you to do so—isn't easy. It takes courage, humility, and faith. And the results may not always be what you expect. What's considered a "success" in heaven may still be labeled a "failure" here on earth.

But don't let that stop you from attempting what others may view as "stupid things." Welcome that disabled foster child into your home. Talk to the atheist next door about your relationship with God. Accept the job with the smaller salary but bigger eternal dividends. Forgive that wrong that seems unforgivable. Risk doing what God wants you to do, even when the task far surpasses your own abilities. If it didn't, others might miss out on catching a glimpse of God's invisible hand at work. And you could miss out on taking part in the adventure of a lifetime.

2

TAKE A
RETRO
ROAD TRIP

W hat's the difference between a "road trip" and a "car trip"? Attitude. A car trip is simply a means of getting from one place to another in as little time as possible. Before you go to heaven, take as few car trips as possible. They're hard on your nerves and your spinal column. However, don't let that dissuade you from taking an authentic road trip.

Unlike a car trip, a road trip is all about the journey The joy is getting into the car and heading down an unfamiliar road, preferably one far away from the interstate, to see what you can see. No time schedules. No agendas. No speeding tickets. Just looking out the window and stopping to explore when the urge arises. A retro road trip goes a step farther. It means meandering through the miles without the diversion of the radio, CD player, or DVDs for the kids. Instead, it's just you, the open road, and the companionship and conversation of those you love, including your heavenly Father.

If you want to take the ultimate retro road trip, consider driving the Mother Road, as Route 66 is affectionately called. You'll no longer find the route on a map, but www.historic66.com can help you locate portions of the famous road between Chicago and Los Angeles. If you're looking for ideas for trips closer to home, www.roadtripusa.com and www.roadtripamerica.com can help you find funky roadside curiosities and historic small towns worth a visit—or at least a good laugh.

Rediscovering the joy of the journey via automobile can help you learn to do the same in your day-to-day life. The less desperate you are to be entertained every waking minute, the more enjoyment you'll find in the simple things—and the more simply wonderful things you'll begin to notice that God provides along the way.

3

EAT
CHEESECAKE
FOR
BREAKFAST

Okay, so cheesecake is not the breakfast of champions. However, it's also not a biohazardous substance. It's food—not particularly nutritious, but food nonetheless. Your relationship with food can play a big part in your life—and in your health. You can rely on it for comfort or shun it in an attempt to change your body image. You can use it to reward yourself or look at mealtimes as a nutritional battle between good and evil. You can even turn to it, instead of God, for help. The simple fact that you have to eat several times a day, every day of your life, makes what you eat, and why, something worth reflecting on.

God designed your body to require food and water. He could have made you self-sustaining, a creature that needed only air to live. But He chose to make your body dependent on an outside source for survival. Then, He gave you a choice as to how you would fill that need. He provided fruits and vegetables, meat and fish, grains and dairy products. He even provided sugarcane for your cheesecake. And just like everything God made, it was good. However, how you choose to use what God has provided may not always be good.

So eat cheesecake for breakfast, just this once. Use it as a litmus test. See how you feel about breaking all of the nutritional rules. Then talk to God about it. Ask Him to help you balance enjoyment with nutrition and make wise choices as to what, and how much, you put into your mouth. From this day on, right up until you're called home to heaven, feed your body in a way that pleases God—as well as your palate.

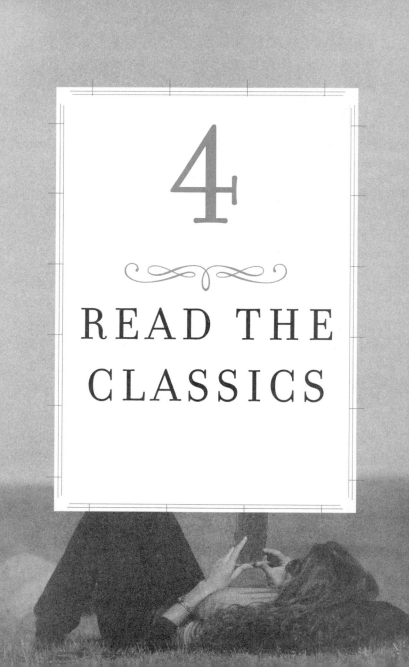

4

READ THE CLASSICS

*T*he *Iliad* and *The Odyssey, War and Peace, To Kill a Mockingbird, Hamlet, Heidi . . .* the libraries and bookstores of the world are filled with titles that have earned the name "classic." What makes something a classic—whether it's a car, a style of furniture, or a book written a couple of centuries ago—is the fact that its appeal transcends time and culture. People of different ages and backgrounds continue to find something about it uniquely satisfying.

When it comes to books, there are more classics to read than there is time to read them before you get to heaven. But don't let that stop you from getting started. If reading is not your favorite pastime, give it another try. In this fast-paced world of sound bites, multitasking, and instant messaging, doing something that requires you to sit down and focus for an extended length of time can increase your attention span while it expands your mind.

Begin by making your own personal list of classics. These may be titles others have recommended or ones that simply pique your interest. Read book reviews in your Sunday paper and peruse the shelves of your local Christian bookstore for new titles to add to your list. Then, make room for some one-on-one time with your chosen classic. Try turning off the TV, stepping away from your e-mail, and picking up a book during your free time. If a book doesn't grab you in the first fifty pages, put it down and move on to another title. Life's too short to waste on books that don't move or challenge you. Finally, ponder what you read. Ask yourself: *What did I learn? What did I like most? Disagree with most fervently? Is there any truth I can apply to my life? What does God think about what I read?* Before you know it, you may find yourself hoping heaven has a library the size of the solar system.

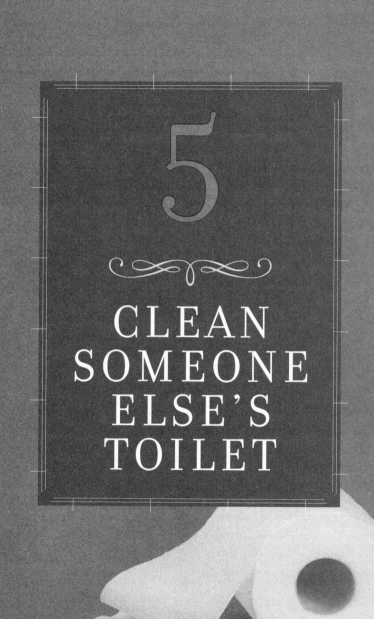

5

CLEAN SOMEONE ELSE'S TOILET

On the road to heaven, there are some potholes—unpleasant jobs that are part of living in this not-yet-perfect world. Some people try to avoid them. Others grit their teeth and dive right in. Still others delegate, not because they can't do what's needed, but because they won't. They feel "dirty jobs" such as these are not worthy of their time. Occasionally there are people who break all the conventional rules. They not only do their own dirty jobs, but they volunteer to help others with theirs. The sense of community, service, and sacrifice these people share captures a little of the spirit of your future home in heaven.

Go ahead and be one of these "oddballs" here on earth. (You'll fit right in when you get to heaven!) Volunteer to clean someone else's toilet. Wash dishes at a homeless shelter. Dig latrines at a church camp. Help with disaster relief in a third-world country . . . not because you have to, but because you want to love others in practical, personal, Christlike ways.

When Jesus washed the feet of His disciples at the Last Supper, He was doing a "dirty" job. Cleaning off the dust, dung, and sweat from sandaled feet was something only servants were expected to do. But Jesus loved His followers so much that He was willing to put their comfort and needs before His own. That's what real love is all about.

What you do to serve others isn't as important as the heart with which you do it. The amazing thing is that once you start serving others, you'll find that even a "dirty" job won't feel dirty anymore. It may still be challenging, tedious, or tiring, but the satisfaction you'll receive by helping others will make it feel more like a blessing than a chore—nothing like a pothole at all.

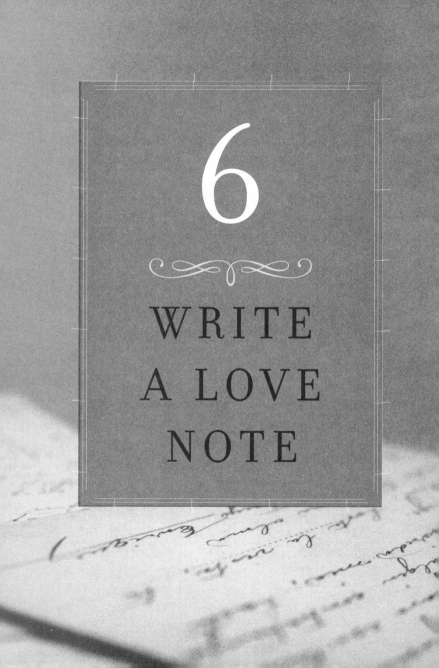

6

WRITE A LOVE NOTE

Words have power. They can encourage, comfort, and heal. They can also wound, cut, and destroy. In the course of a lifetime, most people will undoubtedly be recipients of both healing and hurting comments. Unfortunately, words that wound usually seem to be heard more loudly, and taken more seriously, than those that build up. It's even been said that people need ten affirmations to help them handle every one criticism they receive. You can help add to the "affirmation accounts" of others by always being vocal about how much you care for them. After all, there's no more powerful affirmation in the world than being told you are loved.

However, you can go a step farther by putting your love in print. Writing love notes is one practical way of helping your affirmations become stronger and last longer. Unlike the spoken word that fades away as soon as it's been verbalized, the written word allows the one who "hears" it to enjoy its message again and again. That means a single love note has the potential to cancel out countless criticisms.

On the way to heaven, everyone could use some honest affirmations. You can help fill this need by taking a few moments to write down what you love most about the people closest to your heart. Tell your spouse, your kids, your family, your friends, your coworkers—even those you've never met but have come to respect or admire for some reason—what a difference they've made in your life. Write about what makes them unique in God's world. List specific things you enjoy about them. Describe the depth and breadth of your love. You don't have to be a poet. Just sincerely share what you feel. Your love note may be just the thing someone you care about needs to fill his or her affirmation account to overflowing.

7

GET COMFORTABLE IN YOUR OWN SKIN

When you get a new pair of shoes, the only way to make them comfortable is to break them in. The same goes for your body. God has given you a one-of-a-kind physical form. He wove it together just for you and created it to reflect His glorious image. God intertwined both beauty and wonder into it, inside and out. But your body is not an art object to be put on a pillar and admired. It's a tool that the real you, the eternal part of you that loves and creates and hopes and dreams and worships, uses while you're on this earth. Once you get to heaven, you'll receive a new body—one that won't break down or wear out. But you're not there yet. So the more comfortable you are in the body you have right now, the better you'll be able to use it and enjoy it as each day here on earth unfolds.

You don't break in a body by mistreating it. You need to take care of it, like any tool, so it can do its job well and last a long time. You break in a body by getting off the couch and becoming active whenever you get the chance. Get down on the floor and play with a child. Use your muscles to help your new neighbors move into their house. Put on a swimsuit and get some exercise, no matter what size that swimsuit is. Jump and skip and lift and kneel, even if you jiggle and wiggle and need help getting up.

The less self-conscious you are, the better job you'll do of breaking in your body and becoming comfortable with who you are and how you're made. So, ask God to help you put your inhibitions aside. Stop comparing yourself to others. Get up and get moving. There are places in this world where only a tool like you can do the job.

8

DO
SOMETHING
THAT
SCARES YOU

What gives you the heebie-jeebies when you even think about doing it? Public speaking? Peeking over the edge of the Grand Canyon? Going to the dentist? Or perhaps your fears are more hidden, buried under self-doubt, old wounds, or a lack of faith resulting in a fear of failure, commitment, or rejection. Whatever your deepest fears may be, they're holding you back from doing and becoming all that God has planned for you before you get to heaven.

Before you can face your fears, you need to know what they are. Ask God to help you get to the root of what you're afraid of. If specific fears don't pop into your mind, consider what stresses you out or makes you angry. These can be secondary signs of fear that can lead back to their source, if you're willing to give them an honest look. Once you know what your fears are, it's time to have a face-off. This doesn't mean you have to jump out of a plane if you're afraid of heights or purchase a pet tarantula if you're arachnophobic. Lean on God and take baby steps. Call the dentist's office to schedule a cleaning. Hold on to a friend's hand and take a quick peek off a balcony. Try something at which you'll probably fail, that no one other than you and God will ever know about.

When you face your fears, you gain a greater freedom to be able to do whatever God asks of you in this life. God often asks people to do things they fear. If you have any doubts, just read the Old Testament. However, God knows people rely on Him most when they know they can't accomplish alone what lies ahead. That's what God wants to remind you of every day until you come face-to-face with Him in heaven. He is near and ready to help. He is greater than anything you fear.

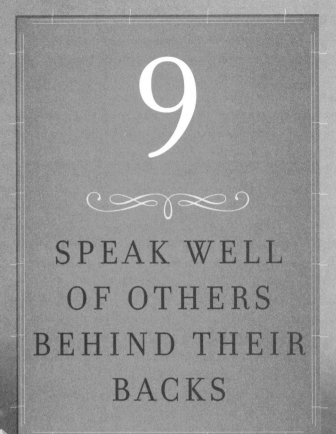

9

SPEAK WELL
OF OTHERS
BEHIND THEIR
BACKS

Y ou have the power to change the course of a conversation. The question is, will you use your power for good or for evil? It's the question all superheroes must face. And in God's world, you do have super powers. Through the power of God's Spirit, you can do what once seemed impossible. You can break a lifelong habit, forgive those who've hurt you, and speak one-on-one with the Creator of the universe. You can also speak well of others behind their backs.

This isn't a naturally human thing to do, but asking God to help you make a habit of it can yield supernatural results. The next time you're with friends who start to gossip, who begin berating someone who's not even there to defend himself or herself or tell "the rest of the story," ask God to help you see this person through His eyes. Every individual is someone God dearly loves. Look for the good in him or her instead of the bad. Share what you can about this person that's positive. The conversation may turn around at that very minute. If not, go a step further by simply saying, "You know what? We don't know the whole story. Let's talk about something else."

Once you start focusing on the positive instead of the negative, you'll begin to see a lot more good in those around you. Look for it. Ask God to help you find it. When you see it, be vocal in telling people what you appreciate in them. Then, build them up to others behind their backs instead of tearing them down. Until you get to heaven, you'll continually be in the company of imperfect people, including yourself. But you can choose to love in a way that more closely resembles the spirit of your future home. With God, you have the power.

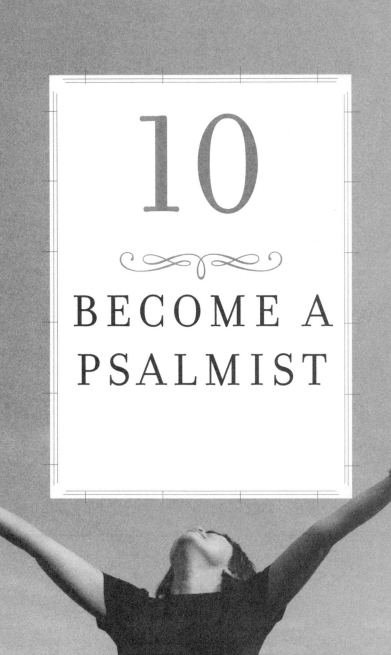

10

∽⟨⟩∽

BECOME A
PSALMIST

T he dictionary defines a psalm as "a sacred song or poem of praise." But don't let that scare you. You don't need to be musically inclined or a rhyming whiz to write a psalm. All you need is a heart that longs to communicate with God. Chances are that everyone will be a psalmist in heaven. The choruses of praise will never end. But there's no reason you can't start that thanksgiving celebration a little early.

Begin by taking a look at the book of Psalms in the Bible. Read a few random chapters. Savor them. Say them aloud. You'll find that what characterizes the prayers in this book is the raw emotion with which the ancient psalmists talk to God. The psalmists' words are so unedited, so authentic, so very human. They share the details of what's going on in their lives—the good, the bad, and the ugly. They ask for God's help and complain when they feel He isn't listening. They're honest and open about experiencing the mountaintop highs of victory and the deep canyon lows of despair. They reiterate the many ways God has come through for them in the past. They whine about how tough things are in the present. They voice their dreams for the future. And they tie everything together with ribbons of praise.

Through a roller coaster of circumstance and emotion, the psalmists remain close enough to God to be awestruck with wonder. When was the last time that happened to you? Risk letting it happen again. Draw close to God in prayer. Speak to Him in a whisper, a shout, or a groan. Share your emotions, your questions, your praise. Then write down how your heart responds to His presence. Make what you write a gift you give directly back to Him. If you're really daring, you might even sing out the words. God doesn't care about the words or the tune as much as He does about the heart of the psalmist who's created them.

11

CELEBRATE A
TRADITIONAL
BRITISH TEA

In the early 1800s, people in Great Britain ate only two meals a day. Breakfast was served midmorning and usually consisted of beef, bread, and ale. Dinner was an elaborate affair served late in the evening that could go on for hours. Anna, the duchess of Bedford, wanted to relieve herself of the light-headed feeling she had as she waited for dinner, so she had her servants prepare a light afternoon meal of finger foods accompanied by the British beverage of choice, a pot of hot tea.

Soon the duchess's idea caught on with the public. Teahouses cropped up all over Great Britain. Here women could dine with their female friends unescorted. The menu of dainty crustless sandwiches, baked goods accompanied by jam and clotted cream, and steaming pots of tea with milk remained the same as Anna's. However, the purpose of "taking tea" began to change. What began as a practical way to ward off hunger pains turned into a time-tested British tradition where conversation with friends became the real main course. Purpose to experience it yourself at least once before you go to heaven.

A crustless cucumber sandwich may never take the place of a Rueben, but celebrating a traditional tea with close friends is a wonderful way to spend an afternoon. It's also a great reminder that tradition can be a positive thing. In today's society, tradition is often looked down on as something that's practiced mindlessly or continued solely because "it's always been done that way." But every tradition began with a purpose.

That holds true for traditions within the church as well. Behind every tradition is a story . . . a reason for baptism, Communion, and treating Sundays as a "day of rest." If you feel you are simply going through the motions of any tradition, discover how it came about. Do a little research. Perhaps over a cup of tea.

12

❧⟫⟨❧

RECORD
YOUR LIFE
STORY

You have a story that is unequaled throughout history. It's a story that's meant to be told, as well as lived. It holds lessons learned, challenges met, and glimpses of God's glory. It's not a perfect tale. No human story is. It contains both good and evil, joy and sadness, faith and doubt, success and failure, triumph and tragedy. But no matter how many ups and downs your story holds, it also holds a priceless treasure: power. With God's help, your story has the power to change another's life while it helps you better understand God's purpose for you here on earth.

You can record your story in lots of ways. You can write a detailed biography or keep a journal that focuses on life-changing moments in your life. You can tape your thoughts about your past, present, and future as you drive to work. What's important is taking the time to look at your life here on earth from two perspectives, your own as well as God's. Look back. Search for God's fingerprints through it all. Look for instances when God taught you priceless lessons through struggle or surprised you with moments of unexpected joy. Consider how you've changed over the last ten, twenty, or thirty years. Do any recurring "themes" continually run through your life? Are there any significant corners you've turned—or keep refusing to turn? Is there anything you'd like to write into your story before you get to heaven?

As God reveals to you how He has worked through your life, share that story with others. Ask God for discernment in knowing what to say and when to say it. Be brief. Be clear. And point others toward God instead of toward your own accomplishments. Your life story can become a living gospel, an account of God at work in the world.

13

GIVE AWAY
SOMETHING
VALUABLE

I f you had to evacuate your home and had one hour to pack your car with everything that was valuable to you (above and beyond your family, pets, and old tax returns!), what would you choose to save? Make a mental list. Then consider why these possessions are so important to you.

Sometimes, items are of value simply because of the memories they represent . . . the funky teacup your best friend gave you, the seashell you brought back from the best vacation ever, the drawing your daughter made in preschool, the wedding photos in which you and your spouse look as if you've barely entered puberty. You may consider these items priceless, but they have no intrinsic value other than being touchstones to the past.

On the other hand, some of the possessions that own a piece of your heart may be more tied up in self-centeredness than sentiment. Perhaps the stereo system you saved for. The necklace you dropped hints for. The dream car you worked overtime for. It may even be the home that houses all of your prized possessions. The truth is, when you go to heaven, none of these things will be going with you. So why not start loosening your grip on them a little early?

You don't need to start big. Donate something to charity that's not broken or worn out. Maybe it no longer holds your interest, but someone else would be thrilled with it. Give something to another family simply because they need it more than you do. You don't need to turn your home into a hollow shell; God never said owning things was wrong. However, He did say it was harder for a rich man to get into heaven than for a camel to fit through the eye of a needle. The less tightly you hold on to your possessions, the more contentment you'll have here on earth.

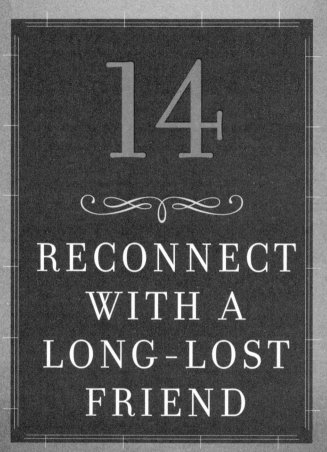

14

RECONNECT WITH A LONG-LOST FRIEND

If you misplaced a hundred-dollar bill, chances are you'd turn your home upside down to find it. But when friends get misplaced along the road of life, all too often their names are simply crossed off the Christmas list and delegated to conversations that begin with, "I wonder what ever happened to . . . " This kind of response does not reflect the true value of friendship. And chances are, neither does it reflect the depth of your true feelings.

Don't let an address change or the passing of time erase someone from your life. Invest in future joy by reconnecting with people from your past. Conduct your own friendship "search and rescue" by typing a friend's name into your favorite search engine. See if any info pops up. Call mutual friends and ask the "Do you know whatever happened to . . . " question. Look through online phone books. Send a note to a friend's last known address, asking whoever currently lives there for help.

Once you think you've located your friend, drop him or her a note. Share a few favorite memories, a little about what's happened in your life since you last saw each other, and discuss your desire to reconnect, even briefly, in person or via phone or e-mail. Chances are, your friend will be as excited to reconnect with you as you are with him or her. However, if you don't hear anything, try one more time. People you care about might be struggling with hard times that they are hesitant to talk about, but they could be times in which they really need a friend who won't give up on them. Your timing in tracking them down may be God's timing in meeting a need.

It takes time, energy, and love to make a friend. Don't squander that investment. Keep others informed of your own change of address, e-mail, or phone number. And when friends do wind up "missing," don't wait until heaven to reconnect with them. Reach out now. True friends are treasures whose value increases with time.

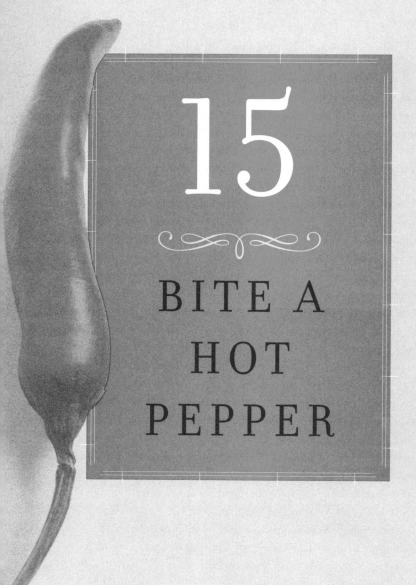

15

❦

BITE A
HOT
PEPPER

A hot chili pepper isn't something that's consumed mindlessly, like popcorn at a movie. It's a whole-body experience that wakes up your taste buds and possibly your tear ducts. You may not think that one little pepper has much in the way of nutritional value, but its thirteen tiny calories provide you with 83 percent of your minimum daily requirement of Vitamin C and a whopping 174 percent of your Vitamin A. Though it's rather high in sodium, it's low in saturated fat and is a good source of dietary fiber. It also packs a powerful punch for your palate. You may love it. You may hate it. But chances are, you won't remain neutral about your encounter with it.

The next time a chili pepper comes with your pizza or lies perched on your antipasto platter, don't just regard it as decoration. Chomp into it for exploration. If munching chilies is already a habit, bite into something else that's foreign to your taste buds— like tripe or haggis. As Mom used to say, "One bite won't kill you!" Mom was right. She knew that a lot of dishes kids turn up their noses at make for pretty good eating. And her reprimand holds as much value for adults as it does for kids.

It's easy to get into a nutritional rut. The more you eat the same old thing, the more likely it is you'll forget to really taste and enjoy what God provides—and to thank Him for it with a sincere heart. When you put something new into your mouth, you pay attention to what's going on in there. You test the texture and flavor. Then you decide if it's worth taking bite number two. Use a chili pepper test run to jump-start a new healthy habit—that of being wholly present when you eat. Take small bites. Chew slowly. Taste and enjoy. Then give God wholehearted thanks.

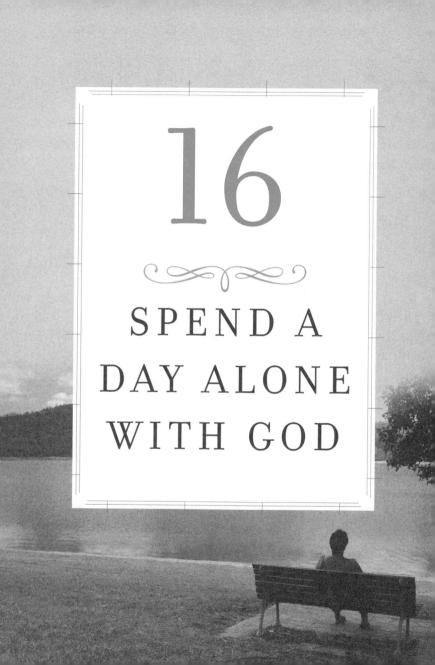

16

SPEND A DAY ALONE WITH GOD

uppose God gives you seventy years to live on this earth. That means, before your departure to heaven, you would have 25,550 days to explore, enjoy, and make a difference in the world around you. Out of all those days of opportunity and adventure, dedicating a single day to spend totally focused on the One who gave you the gift of life itself seems like a small thing. And it is, especially in light of eternity.

Don't let the fear of the unknown scare you off from spending time with the One you love. Take out your calendar. Draw a big heart over the next free day you find and write "God + me" in the center of it. Chances are, things will come up that will tempt you to put off your day with God, so regard it as you would any appointment scheduled with a dear friend. Safeguard the time.

When the day arrives, treat it as a celebration. Gather your Bible, your journal (or a notebook), a pen, and a sack lunch. Get away from familiar surroundings. Head to a beautiful, secluded spot. If the weather is good, head for the outside. If not, you can spend time with God right in your car.

There's no set itinerary when spending time with a friend. Begin as you would with anyone you love—chat about what's going on in your life. From there, read from the book of Psalms or the Gospel of John. Write down everything you feel God is impressing on your heart about your life and your relationship with Him. Sing. Pray, both out loud and silently. Listen. Dream. Even falling asleep while you're talking to God is not a bad thing. He'll still be there, ready to continue your conversation as soon as you awake. And when your time is finished, get out your date book. Chances are you'll want to schedule some time away with God again in the near future.

17

❧◦⟳⟲◦❧

GO
HOME
AGAIN

With a little planning, you can go home again. Best of all, you can invite God along for the ride. It's a journey worth taking before you make that final change of address to your home in heaven. That's because visiting the place where you grew up can remind you of what it's like to be a kid. It can help you remember what mattered and what you overlooked, who loved you and whom you loved in return, or how it felt to be small in a great big world.

If you moved frequently as a child, plan a pilgrimage to visit as many former addresses as you can. If your childhood home is now a high-rise apartment or a vacant lot, get as close as you can to where you actually lived. If you have the good fortune of being able to see the actual residence that was home to many of your childhood memories, dare to knock on the door. Explain who you are and ask if you can go inside. Be sure to make clear that you're not there to judge anyone's housekeeping or decorator skills. If you have kids of your own, take them along. Not only will it make homeowners feel more at ease about allowing you onto their property, it will help your children better understand that you really were a kid once upon a time—and it will remind you of what it felt like to be at the same stage in life as your children are now.

After your visit, spend some time journaling. Record how you felt stepping back in time. Write down any specific events in your childhood that your visit brought to mind. Consider how these events helped shape who you are today. Take time to laugh, cry, reflect, pray . . . whatever you need to do. Then, ask God to show you where and when His hand was at work in your childhood, especially in places that may have gone unnoticed before. After all, He was there all the time, as big as ever, even when you were small.

18

VISIT
THE MALL
WITHOUT
SPENDING A
DIME

The world is filled with stuff. Your local mall is one place where lots of this stuff lives. It cries out from store windows and displays, "You want me! You need me! I'll make you beautiful! I'll make your life simpler. I'll make you happy. Promise!" But stuff, no matter how valuable, useful, or beautiful, is still just stuff. Purchasing something can provide a temporary lift for your spirits, but it has no power to fill an empty life. Only God can do that. In the meantime, all the stuff you buy comes with a price tag that is more than financial. Once you own something, you have to wash it, dust it, repair it, and in all probability, one day garage-sale it.

While you're here on earth, practice traveling light. Learn how to appreciate stuff without having to own it. Make a game of it. If you enjoy shopping with friends or checking out the latest gadgets at the electronics store, do it with the same attitude you would have in approaching a museum. If you went to the Louvre or the Smithsonian, you'd see things that would capture your imagination. Art that would look great in your family room. Historical artifacts that would grace a bookshelf with style. Beautiful clothing once worn by famous people that may actually be your size. But you know this stuff is inaccessible to you. You can enjoy looking at it without longing to whip out your credit card.

You can do the same thing at the mall. When you actually need something, great. Make an informed purchase. But if you feel you need something only after you see it, chances are your need is only a want. You can still enjoy looking at stuff. Appreciate its design and workmanship. Even marvel at its price. Then, put it down, walk away, and enjoy all that God has graciously given you already.

19

❦

TOUCH AN
UNTOUCHABLE

In the Hindu caste system, some people are viewed as "untouchable." These individuals are deemed intrinsically inferior from the womb to the grave. Although the caste system is illegal in India, its practices are still widely accepted. Members of the lowest caste are still regularly shunned, insulted, and oppressed. You may breathe a sigh of relief or feel a twinge of superiority because you don't believe anyone's untouchable. Or do you?

Take a good look at how you feel about different groups of people. Bikers. Manual laborers. Teenagers. Panhandlers. The elderly. Unwed mothers. Immigrants. People with AIDS. Criminals. Police officers. Politicians. Truckers. The physically handicapped. People with tattoos and body piercings. Individuals with a different skin color, religion, or even gender—to name just a few. Next consider people who simply rub you the wrong way, people whom you try to avoid spending time with at all costs. The groups of people or individuals whom you feel inclined to turn away from make up your own personal "untouchable" list.

Before you get to heaven, banish any internal caste system that's preventing you from opening your hands and your heart to others. The best way to begin is with prayer. Ask God to bring situations into your life that will allow you to get close enough to reach out and "touch" an untouchable. You may feel uncomfortable at first. You may even feel like a hypocrite, that your actions are not sincere. But the desire to do the right thing can be a genuine motivation for love. The more you put your love into action, the easier it will be to see how God has woven His image into each and every person, making it impossible for anyone to ever be an "untouchable."

20

~~~
❦
~~~

READ THE
BIBLE FROM
COVER TO
COVER

I magine opening your mailbox and finding a love letter from your soul mate. You recognize the handwriting at once and anxiously tear open the envelope. As you enter the front door, you toss the bills, flyers, and junk mail aside before settling down on the couch to take in every word of what your true love has to say. But you notice the letter is rather long. The print is small. And some of the verbiage is—to put it bluntly—hard to understand. You know that every word has been chosen with care and written especially for you, but you decide to read the opening greeting and the last paragraph and call it quits. After all, you've gotten the gist of the letter. You have more important things to do with your time. Like check out the junk mail on the coffee table.

If you haven't read the Bible from cover to cover, that's exactly what you've done with it. You've skimmed a love letter that has the power to change your life and your heart. Before you go to heaven, get to know the One who's waiting there for you. The Bible introduces you to God's character, how He works in the world, and His plan for your life here on earth and in heaven. Every word carries His fingerprint. Every verse reveals His truth.

Get acquainted with each and every chapter of the Old and the New Testament. You don't have to read every book sequentially, beginning with page one. Mix them up. Many study-Bibles contain a schedule that can help you read through the Bible in a year. A good study Bible will also provide insight into why, when, by whom, and to whom a book was written. However, the ultimate study aid is God's very own Spirit. Ask God to help you understand and apply what you're reading. The better picture you have of who God is, the deeper your love for Him will grow.

21

❦

WEAR THE SIZE THAT FITS

For some people, the little label inside their clothing really plays havoc with their self-image. If you're one of these people, don't let a number label you. Refuse to buy anything other than the size that fits. When you're shopping for clothing, try on several sizes of the same item. Bend over. Sit down. Stand in front of the mirror and check out the fit, front and back. Then, buy only what fits you well, regardless of whether it's your usual size or not. Wearing things that don't fit properly leaves you pulling, tugging, and uncomfortable throughout the day. In other words, they distract you from what's really important in life. So, wear the size that fits, without apologies.

However, if the reason you're tempted to wear a different size is that you'd rather be a different size, look at something other than the number on the label. Look at your lifestyle. If you're unhappy with your size because it's a side effect of living an unhealthy lifestyle, then you need to take positive action. Don't let bad habits rob you of the joy God has for you before you get to heaven. Call your doctor and begin taking steps toward changing your life, and your size, one day at a time.

But if you're at a healthy weight for your height and still discontented with your size, it's time to look at your heart instead of the label on your jeans. There is not one "perfect" size when it comes to the human body. God designed people in all different heights and builds. If you aren't happy with the choice He's made for you, it's time for a heart-to-heart chat. Talk to Him about why your size matters so much to you. Allow Him to help you discover your true beauty, a beauty that will last throughout eternity—in a place where size never matters.

22

PURSUE A DREAM

All of us have a few dreams we'd like to see become reality before we go to heaven. These could be dreams that began in childhood, dreams such as becoming a rock star, an astronaut, or a parent. They could also be dreams we've picked up along the road of life as we've aged. Dreams to climb Mount Everest, master paint with watercolors, run a marathon, pet a whale, or visit the Eiffel Tower. Whatever our most cherished dreams may be, they reveal a bit of what our hearts are like, a bit of who God created us to be.

Wanting to pursue these dreams isn't selfish. It's a natural, God-inspired desire. However, how you choose to pursue these dreams will depend on what other realities God has woven into your life through the years. Dreams are often reshaped and revised as you grow older. You may find that what's at the heart of your longing to become a rock star is fulfilled simply by taking guitar lessons, singing karaoke on the weekends, or joining the church choir. Your dream of becoming a parent may come true by volunteering to be a Big Brother or Big Sister in your community. Your dream of climbing Mount Everest may be satiated by taking a one-day hike up Pike's Peak.

Dreams don't usually come true all at once. They become reality step-by-step—not with the wave of a magic wand, but with planning, effort, and commitment. If you feel that petting a whale is a God-given desire, one that stirs something deep in your soul, do something about it. In your spare time, read books on whales. Watch the nature channel. Research what it would take to book a trip to Victoria, British Columbia; Cabo San Lucas, Mexico; or Churchill, Canada, where you can get up close and personal with one of these gentle giants. Then plan, save, and go. Your dream-come-true will help you better understand the nature of your heart, as well as God's heart toward you, in a new and wonderful way.

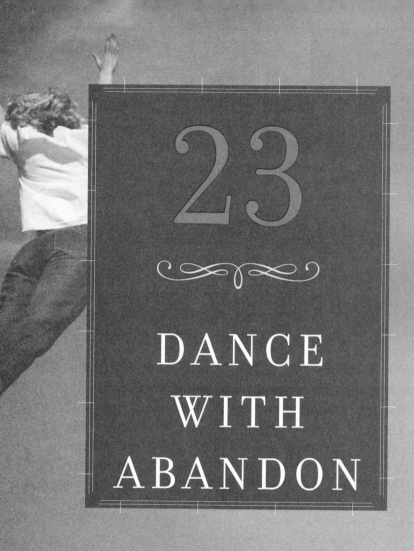

23

DANCE
WITH
ABANDON

Polka, samba, hip-hop, salsa, waltz . . . or just put on some music and get your body moving to the beat. Dancing is fun, freeing, and good for your health. While you can learn plenty of formal steps, simply getting into the habit of being able to respond to music in a physical way is something worth doing before you get to heaven. After all, there will be plenty of dancing there. In the same way that David danced before God to express his joy and gratitude, you'll get your chance to dance with abandon before the Lord in heaven. Best get into practice here and now!

The biggest barrier to dancing is the fear of looking silly. It's true that some people have a better sense of rhythm than others. But you don't have to be a Fred Astaire or Ginger Rogers to get up and sway. If just reading this makes your stomach tense and your palms sweat, it's time to put down this book and turn on the stereo. The best way to begin is to choose some music that helps you feel close to God. It could be a CD of praise songs or a classical symphony that always moves you to tears. Whatever you choose, just start the music, close your eyes, and allow your body to respond to what you hear. Forget about how you look or whether or not you're doing it "wrong." Just listen, move, and worship God without words. Whatever "dance" you do will be beautiful in God's eyes.

The more you get comfortable dancing before God, the easier it will be to relax and enjoy dancing as a recreational pastime. Who knows? You may discover there's a Fred or Ginger inside you who's been waiting for the opportunity to cut a rug and shine.

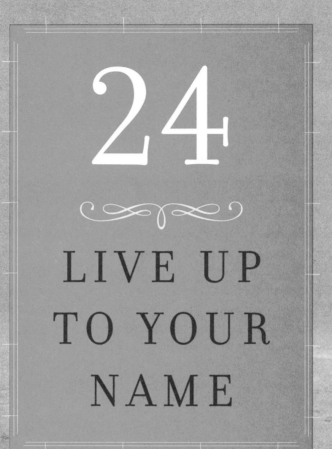

24

LIVE UP
TO YOUR
NAME

Your name is more than what you're known by. It's your calling card. You may love the way it rolls off your tongue or wish your parents had been a little more, or less, creative in selecting your personal moniker. But whatever your name happens to be, it has a meaning. Probably more than one, if you look at derivations of it used around the world.

To live up to the name you've been given, it's helpful to know what it means. Search the Internet or books of baby names to discover the history and significance of your given name. Write down what seems to apply to you. Look it over. Think about it. Pray over it. Then, ask God what you should do with what you've learned. For instance, if your name is Victor, pray for the wisdom and strength you need to live life more "victoriously." If your name is Katherine, ask God to show you what areas of your life need to change so you can truly be a "pure one."

In biblical times, people's names were an integral part of who they were. That's why God sometimes changed them, as shown in the Bible. Once people turned to Him, the direction of their lives, and the essence of who they were, came more into line with who God created them to be. Hence, Abram (which means "exalted father") became Abraham (meaning "father of many").

God has a special name picked out just for you. It may be the one you go by now, or it may not be revealed until you meet your Father face-to-face in heaven. Either way, you can begin to live out your "true" name now by staying close to God, talking to Him in prayer, learning more about Him through the Bible, and reaching out in love to others so that His character has a chance to mature in you.

25

PET A
MANTA
RAY

Rays have a bad reputation. They're related to sharks (not the most congenial of sea creatures) and nicknamed "devil fish" because early sailors believed they saw horns protruding from their flat, wing-like bodies. Most people associate all rays with the stingray, one species of ray with poisonous spines on its tail. Although some species can hurt you, the vast majority of the 425 different kinds of rays are harmless. They're also amazingly beautiful, graceful, and people-friendly. What's more, to the touch they feel like breathing velvet.

So before you go to heaven, pet a ray. Don't try this in the wild where you may not know one ray from another and where your touch could subject the ray to infection. However, in carefully monitored touch pools at aquariums and aquatic amusement parks, don't hesitate to get up close and personal with the various rays on display. Not only is watching their watery ballet a treat for the eyes, but petting them gives you a hands-on lesson in "things aren't always as they seem." Your initial reaction to them may be, "Danger! Slimy, predatory creature nearby! Keep your distance!" However, first impressions do not always tell the whole truth.

This holds true for so many encounters in life . . . with opportunities, with people, with heartache, and with God. Sometimes, what you expect is not at all what you get. Getting up close and personal relationally, emotionally, and spiritually can open you up to unexpected joy that you could easily miss if you were to rely solely on first impressions. Allow the glorious, graceful ray to teach you a lesson about living life to the fullest here on earth. Life is like the ocean—there's beauty, mystery, and adventure just below the surface. Risk a personal encounter with it.

26

~⁂~

GROW A
NEW
FRIEND

Every individual is like a flower seed. God chooses what type of one-of-a-kind plant will grow from that seed, as well as the patch of Planet Earth where it will grow best. Some seeds wind up in Mombasa, while others land in Milwaukee. Wherever God plants you, you have the opportunity to get to know, and grow along with, the other burgeoning blooms in your vicinity.

In this friendship garden, you'll always find yourself surrounded by more potential friends than you could ever get to know. And if you have a strong circle of buddies already, it's tempting to put your friendship-making skills on hold and simply enjoy the beautiful blossoms God's previously placed in your life. But by doing that, you could miss out on the friendship of a lifetime, one that extends from this life right into eternity.

So before you go to heaven, reach out and grow a new friend—regularly. The beautiful thing about a circle of friends is that it can always expand to hold one more. Don't let a busy social schedule, shyness, or complacency become an excuse that keeps you from striking up a conversation with a new neighbor, that fellow aerobics enthusiast you keep bumping into at the gym, or even the person sitting next to you on an airplane. You never know when you'll cross paths with someone whose heart resonates with your own. That individual may really need someone exactly like you in his or her life right now, or vice versa.

The most beautiful gardens are well planned. They are sown with a variety of plants that bloom at different times, which helps to keep them looking lush and colorful year round. Continuing to reach out to others in friendship, no matter how "mature" your garden is, will keep your love growing strong season after season, while adding variety and vibrancy to your life.

27

~~~

WATCH A
METEOR
SHOWER

Meteors are a daily occurrence. They're nothing more than specks of dust and ice that range in size from a grain of sand to a common green pea. These "shooting stars" hurtle toward earth at over 158,000 miles per hour and burn up as they enter earth's atmosphere. So why bother staying up past your bedtime in an often chilly and inconvenient location to see a racing speck of dust? Because it's fun—and because the experience has so much to teach you about your place in God's universe.

While you can see a meteor on any clear night, several major showers occur every year. One of the most popular is the Perseids shower, which is visible for several weeks sometime between July 25 and August 18. With an average of seventy meteors an hour, this shower guarantees you'll see some heavenly action. After 11:30 PM, head as far away from city lights as possible, place a blanket on the ground, then lie back and keep your eyes open—as well as your mind. In between "ooohing" and "ahhhing" over streaks of white, red, and green light, you'll have plenty of time to reflect on how big God's universe is and how small you are in comparison.

You and a meteor have a lot in common. After all, the Bible says you really are just a speck of dust. However, God has taken something that could be common, insignificant, and temporary and fashioned you into someone who is unique, precious, and eternal. In light of eternity, your life on earth is as brief as the trail of a meteor. However, that short life can blaze with the brilliance of a shooting star as each day you allow God's light of love to shine through you, making both His power and your own unique beauty more visible to the world.

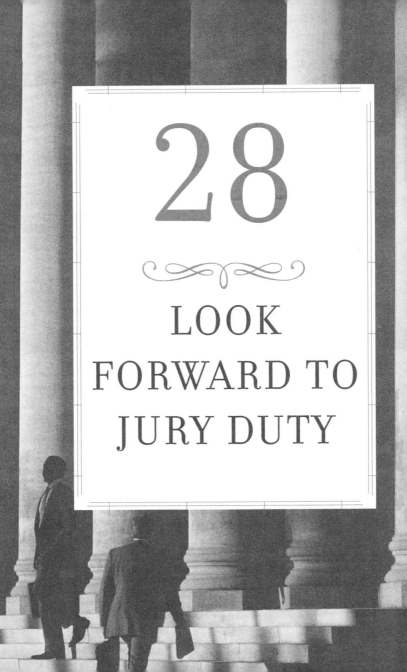

28

LOOK FORWARD TO JURY DUTY

You open the mail and there it is—a summons for jury duty. No matter what the date is on which you're scheduled to appear, it's bound to be inconvenient. That's because you have a life. You have commitments. You have plans. Now, the judicial system is asking you to move things around—to commit yourself for an undetermined time to do unfamiliar things at a courthouse where a parking spot is hard to come by and the traffic is bumper-to-bumper. Then, of course, there's the metal detector and the uncomfortable chairs and the measly couple of dollars a day they offer in compensation . . . well, you could go on and on. Chances are, you usually do.

But what if you were on the other side of that jury, sitting in a chair, accused of something you didn't do? Or what if you were a victim who had to testify, hoping that the one who hurt you would be prevented from doing the same thing to other people? You would want someone to listen to your story, look objectively at the facts, and sift the truth from the lies. You would want someone exactly like you on that jury.

The next time you receive a jury summons, before you roll your eyes or let out a moan, stop and think. Remember that that piece of paper is an invitation to help administer justice. God is a just God. Throughout the Bible He reminds you to help those who are victimized. Jury duty is one of your chances to do just that. You may never make it beyond the waiting room. You may end up debating the legitimacy of a parking ticket. But wherever people's lives are involved—this side of heaven where there is a right and a wrong—God wants you to stand up for what's right. A job such as that is rarely convenient or comfortable. But in light of eternity, it's definitely important.

29

❧❧

BUILD A
SAND
CASTLE

Going to the beach is a given. No one should head to heaven without first having experienced the vastness, power, and mystery of the ocean. Every wave gives glory to God with its thunder, constancy, and grace. However, there's more to the beach than getting your feet wet, scouring for shells, and trying to slather on enough sunscreen to prevent a sunburn. There's also the challenge of building a sand castle.

Building sand castles is not only for kids. A simple sand castle can hold life lessons through leisurely play for even the most refined adults. Begin by digging a hole down to the water table. (The closer you are to the shoreline, the shorter the dig this will be, but the more perilous the waves may be!) Moving quickly, pull the wet sand from the bottom of the hole toward you. Gently flatten large handfuls of sand like you're making tortillas, stacking them on top of each other to form towers. Use smaller handfuls the higher you go, so your castle doesn't become top-heavy. From that point on, let your imagination run free.

If children offer to help you, which they're likely to do, invite them to join in—even if they mess up your architectural masterpiece. Sand-castle building is much more about the process than the actual finished product. Relax, laugh, build up, knock down, mess up, get gritty, and remember not to get too attached to your creation. After all, its destiny is destruction. If you get the chance, return to look at what's left of your work of art after the tide takes its toll. Remember, everything you create or achieve on this earth has the same destiny as your sand castle. The only thing God created that will endure throughout eternity is people. Use every sand castle you see as a reminder that you were built to last.

30

ASK FOR
DIRECTIONS

Men are often given a bad rap about not asking for directions. But many women are guilty of the very same thing. It seems that individuals of both sexes would rather wander aimlessly down unfamiliar streets, risk putting together something the wrong way, or meander through life without God's guidance rather than humble themselves enough to admit there are things they don't know. If you are one of these people, you'll find the road to heaven a lot less bumpy if you admit you need some help along the way.

When you need help, whom or what you turn to makes a big difference. You wouldn't dial operator assistance if you needed to know how to make chicken Marsala or consult a map if you wanted to change the oil in your car. In the same way, if you need help figuring out who you are and what your purpose is in this life, you should turn to the ultimate authority—the One who made you and therefore knows your heart better than anyone else.

Only God is familiar with both you and every twist and turn you will face on the road to heaven. When life is confusing, when you're unsure of which way to go, don't waste your precious days drifting without direction. Call out to God. Pray with an open mind and an open heart. Next, open the Bible. Balance any direction in which you feel led to go with the guidelines that God has already provided. Day by day, as you stay close to God, He'll reveal what direction your next step should take.

As for the little things, such as programming your DVD player or navigating your way to a new restaurant, God has already provided you with directions. They usually come in the form of other people who know more than you do about a particular subject. Humbly lean on their expertise when you need it. God may guide you to help them someday.

31

⌘

GROW
SOMETHING
YOURSELF—
WITH GOD'S
HELP

I t's true that only God can make something grow. You can pre-pare the soil, plant a seed, water it, and even pick the fruit when the season is right, but there is a miracle that happens some-where in between—a miracle that turns one cell into two and more. Everything you eat is a miracle of life and growth somewhere down the line. When you eat something that you've had a hand in growing— something you've waited for, cared for, and worked hand in hand with God for—you're reminded of how very dependent you are on God for the most basic necessities of life.

So grow some herbs in your kitchen window. Plant a fruit tree in your backyard. Join others in gardening a neighborhood vegetable co-op. Then, watch for the miracle. Manna is the only food that ever appeared overnight. Every other food takes time to grow to maturity, whether it's a zucchini in the garden—or even a "hamburger on the hoof." Watching and waiting for what you've planted helps you better appreciate what you pick up at the grocery store. Every item in the produce section, every loaf of bread in the bakery, and every jar of pickles on the shelf is a team effort. The team captain is always God, but countless others are involved in providing you with all the nutri-tious options you have to choose from each day. Allow your gratitude to grow right along with your garden.

Once your own produce has reached the peak of perfection, cele-brate your first bite. In the Old Testament, the "firstfruits" of every harvest were offered to God. You can do the same by offering a heart-felt word of gratitude for your God-given gift of fruit, vegetables, or herbs. It's only through God's grace that they are available at your table. That's why returning a word of "grace" to God at mealtime—or any other time, for that matter—is such an appropriate response.

32

BECOME AN UNDERCOVER ENCOURAGER

Before you go to heaven, do something secret, something only you and God will ever know about. Become an undercover encourager. Ask God to help you choose someone to pour words of encouragement and prayer over. Perhaps it will be an elderly person who spends a lot of time alone. It could be a child struggling with his or her parents' divorce. It might even be someone who isn't very easy to like but who could use some kind words to soften his or her heart. It could be a neighbor, a coworker, or someone at your church who's in need. Whoever it is, risk reaching out.

Begin praying for your "secret pal." Ask God to give you ideas about how to best reach out in love. A great way to begin your adventure as an undercover encourager and still maintain a "secret identity" is to send a card without a signature or return address. Its message could be as simple as "Just wanted to let you know someone's thinking of you and praying for you."

From there on out, let God's Spirit and your creativity lead the way. Keep a stack of greeting cards or blank note cards on hand so you can send a few encouraging words, a Scripture passage, or an inspiring quote or poem every week or so. Leave flowers on the person's doorstep. Send an uplifting book or CD. If there are tangible needs you can fill, find ways to help provide for them—ways that cannot be traced back to you.

Resist the urge to brag to your family or friends about what you're doing. Keep everything you do a secret shared only between you and God. Continue praying regularly and encouraging creatively. You may get to hear secondhand how the little things you've done have made a big difference in your secret pal's life. If you don't have that opportunity here on earth, you can look forward to hearing about it when you get to heaven.

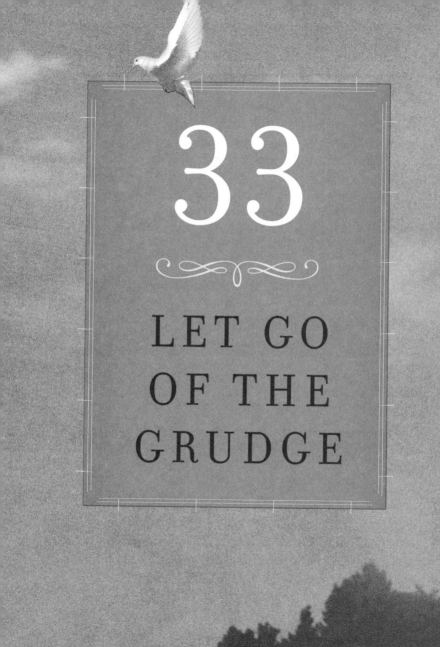

33

LET GO
OF THE
GRUDGE

When you're at your favorite fishing hole, some things you catch are not worth taking home for the fish fry. They are the little guys—the puny fish that you release back into the lake because they're not worth the time and effort it would take to clean them. They are the lucky ones you let off the hook.

Before you go to heaven, do the same for any people against whom you're holding a grudge. Their offenses may be the size of a salmon, a marlin, or even a killer whale. But the truth is that the hook is under your skin, not theirs. Allowing a grudge to eat away at you can leave your whole life smelling like last week's trout. It can affect your attitude, your energy, your emotions, and your example to others. It can even affect your relationship with God. The Bible says that you are to forgive others in the same way that God's forgiven you. Consider all you've done that's worthy of God's turning His back on you. But God's done exactly the opposite. He sent His Son to bear the punishment for your offenses. He's embraced you with open arms and invited you to spend eternity with Him. Learn from His love. You can't extend forgiveness with one hand while carrying a grudge in the other.

The truth is, when it comes to releasing bitterness against someone in your life, you've got bigger fish to fry. Don't waste another minute's energy and emotion on someone who will have to answer to God for what's been done. Learn what you can from the past. Forgive as many times as the offense rises to the surface of your mind. Let go of the grudge. Then, move on to clearer, calmer waters. God has so many adventures ahead of you that you don't want to be distracted by anything that takes your eyes off Him.

34

VISIT
AN ALIEN
ENVIRONMENT

Travel to a place where the laws of gravity refuse to work the way you're accustomed to. Where you float, instead of fall. Where you can't breathe, unless you're carrying supplemental oxygen. Where most of the terrain is virtually unexplored, devoid of footprints or civilization—but not of life. For there you'll find alien life forms in all colors, shapes, and sizes. Another planet? If you happen to be given that opportunity, go for it. But if space travel is beyond your reach, do the next best thing—explore the ocean.

Although 71 percent of the earth's surface is covered by oceans and 80 percent of all life on earth exists there, scientists know less about some of its creatures, vegetation, and landscapes than they do about distant planets. Visiting aquariums or watching a special on the nature channel can give you some great information on the ocean. However, you can't really experience what it's like until you dive in. So snorkel, scuba dive, or take a submarine ride to catch a glimpse of this amazing other world. You can't dive deep enough on your own to uncover all the ocean's mysteries, but even on the most uneventful trip beneath the waves, you will see enough aquatic wonders to make you think.

As you explore, as you watch the alien way in which sea creatures move and breathe, you instantly recognize that they're at home and you're not. In some ways, you are like those creatures of the deep. Although you've adapted to living life on this earth, your true home is in heaven. Like the opalescent piranha, whose color changes to a flat gray once it is removed from the water, your true colors cannot really be seen here on earth. There is more to you, and your life, than what you are experiencing here and now. Let a glimpse of an aquatic, alien world be a reminder that there's a world where wonder and beauty and God Himself are awaiting you, a place where you'll feel truly at home for the very first time.

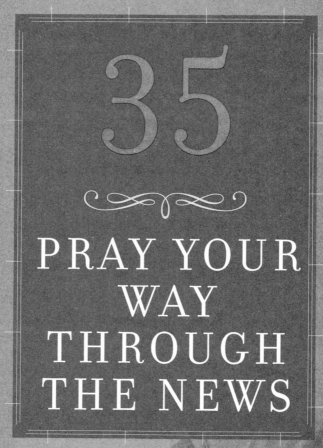

35

PRAY YOUR WAY THROUGH THE NEWS

In a world of instant information, live video feeds, and trying to scoop the competition for better ratings, the news is in danger of becoming little more than entertainment for the masses. A "slow news day" (i.e., one in which there are no murders or national crises) is lamented. A natural disaster immediately becomes fodder for a new "movie of the week." Meanwhile, God weeps.

Disaster, tragedy, depravity, poverty, war, famine . . . the things that make headlines should do more than hold your interest. They should drive you to your knees. Today when you pick up the morning paper or turn on the evening news, look beyond the weather forecast and sports scores. Look deeper than the sensational headlines and latest scientific discoveries. Look past the sound bites to the individuals who are living within the headlines. Put yourself in their shoes. Then put their lives into God's hands through prayer.

In heaven there will be no tears. But that's not the story here on earth. Being vulnerable enough to allow your own heart to break over what breaks God's heart will deepen your capacity for empathy and compassion. As that compassion beckons you to turn to God for help, you have the privilege of working hand in hand with the God of the universe to make a positive difference in others' lives. Through the mystery of prayer, invite God to act on behalf of those you do not have the power to assist on your own. Whether the people on the news live on the other side of town or around the world, your heartfelt prayers can help supply comfort, wisdom, protection, healing, and aid. Although your "relief effort" will never make the evening news, it will affect the lives of others in ways you may never know about until you reach your home in heaven.

36

DYE YOUR
HAIR

Change is good—or so the saying goes. But change can also be downright scary, especially when you feel comfortable with the status quo. Before you get to heaven, risk shaking things up a bit here on earth. Challenge your concept (and everyone else's) of who you are. Go ahead. Dye your hair.

You don't have to go permanent—or purple. And if your knees start to quake at the very thought, try a colored rinse that fades away after a few washes. Feel free to experiment. After all, this isn't a tattoo. Hair keeps on growing. Dying your hair is like changing your clothes. You just end up "wearing the same outfit" for a while.

Changing your hair color can challenge you to grab hold of the fact that you are not your appearance. You are not your hair color, your height, your skin tone, or the size of your clothes. You, the real you, is the one who lives inside all the trappings of your form and fashion. The more dependent your self-image is on your appearance, and on how others perceive you, the harder it will be for you to make a radical color change—unless of course, you're "follicly challenged" (i.e., bald) or have been dying your hair for so long you can hardly remember what your real color is. If you already dye your hair, consider going *au naturel* for a few months. And if you're bald, well, there's always that tattoo.

It could be said that even God welcomes a change in your hair color. After all, He designed your hair to turn gray as you age. And not one of those gray hairs makes you any less beautiful in His eyes. That's because God sees you from the inside out. He cares about whether your heart is right, not whether your hair has just the right color, body, and shine. So shake up your body image a bit. It just may help you catch a glimpse of yourself through God's eyes.

37

∽≋∽

UNPLUG
FOR A DAY

If the power went out at your house for a day, what would you miss most? Suppose your phone lines, cell phone, pager, and wireless Internet all went kaput as well, not to mention any other little handheld gadget you happen to have lying around. How would it change how you spend your time? At some point before your sojourn on earth ends, give yourself the chance to find out. Choose to live life unplugged for a day.

This is not an exercise in roughing it. It's more of an invitation to recognize that you have options in this life, choices that you may have forgotten you could make in a world filled with ringing cell phones, hissing cappuccino makers, and pounding stereo systems. You can choose to live a simpler life, one where you don't have to be tethered to a cell phone, a blow-dryer, or a television set every day. You don't need to purchase every new gadget and gizmo that finds its way to your local electronics superstore. You can slow down the pace, turn down the noise, and reduce the cost of living by unplugging every now and then.

Try it out for twenty-four hours. Make your own music instead of turning on the radio. Play board games instead of video games. Chat instead of putting on a DVD. Melt marshmallows in the family room fireplace to make s'mores for dessert. Send a letter instead of an e-mail. Put on a sweater instead of turning up the heat, or make a fan out of a piece of paper to stir a breeze when the temperature rises. Discover the natural ambiance of spending the evening by candlelight. Convenience and comfort are great, but they are not essential for living a joy-filled life. Once you rediscover some of life's simpler pleasures, you may actually look forward to the next time the power goes out.

38

❧❧❧

WALK IN
JESUS'
FOOTSTEPS

Two thousand years ago, Jesus walked this earth. He laughed, cried, slept, wept, prayed, loved, and offered up His life so you could have a future home in heaven. One way you can get to know Jesus better before you meet Him face-to-face is to visit the place here on earth He called home. A visit to Israel is a great way to make the Bible come alive in your mind. Step back into history and view the same vistas Jesus saw. Dip your toe into the Jordan where He was baptized. Sail on the Sea of Galilee where He walked on water. Pray over the city of Jerusalem just as Jesus once did through tears. Break a loaf of freshly baked bread and remember Him.

Although the exact locations of Jesus' birth, death, and burial are up for debate, the fact that these events really happened is as certain as the fact that you're reading these words today. Seeing first-hand the part of the world where God walked this earth will help you put flesh and blood on the frame of familiar gospel stories.

If, however, traveling to Israel is something that proves impossible because of physical, financial, or political concerns, the next best thing to wandering the streets of Jerusalem is taking a slow, thoughtful, walk through the Gospels themselves. Digest one miraculous event or parable at a time. Picture yourself in the crowd witnessing a miracle, as a disciple leaving your fishing net behind, as Jesus' mother watching her Son die on the cross, as Mary Magdalene discovering an angel at Jesus' empty tomb. Allow God's Spirit to be your travel guide as you journey through Jesus' life on earth. Then, walk in Jesus' footsteps here and now by letting His example of compassion, forgiveness, mercy, and grace change the way you learn, live, and love.

39

GIVE YOUR HEART AWAY TO A CHILD

Children are dependent, self-centered, creative, and trusting. They can laugh over almost anything, love almost anybody, and fall asleep almost anywhere. They are some of God's most entertaining and enjoyable teachers in this life. But to really learn from them, you need to get close to them. Close enough to give your heart away.

You don't have to be a parent to connect with a child in a life-changing way. And being a parent doesn't automatically mean you've allowed yourself to learn from and wholly love a child. But whether or not this is something you've done before, giving your heart away to a kid is a great prelude to heaven. Of course, this means you'll have to actually spend time with a child. If one isn't living in your home at the moment, volunteer to work in your church's nursery, or babysit for a friend. But don't settle for simply being a caregiver. Become an avid student and friend.

Play together. Listen. Watch. Learn. The Bible says that unless you become like a child, you'll never get to heaven. Grab hold of the truth behind these words. Rediscover the beauty and power of innocence, humility, sincerity, passion, and faith. Catch glimpses of unconditional love and unbridled joy. But don't study the child you're spending time with like a scientific specimen. Risk showering him or her with love. Understand, that's not synonymous with showering a child with gifts, unless those gifts are ones that can be held in the heart instead of in human hands. And be forewarned that really loving a child will probably expose you to disappointment, frustration, and anger, as well as joy. But that's part of what giving your heart away involves. Just talk to your heavenly Father about what loving you has cost Him. Then, ask Him if it was worth it. Once you give your heart away to a child, your answer will echo God's.

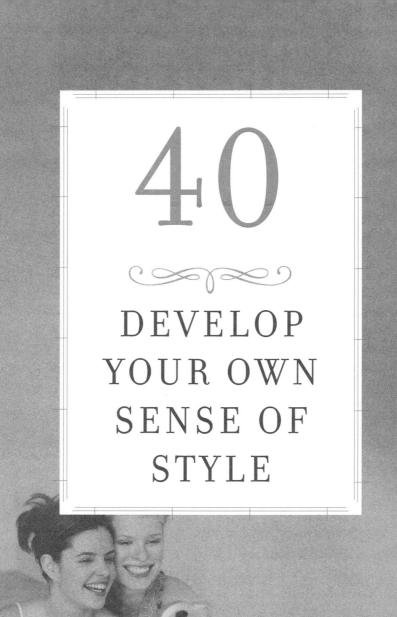

40

DEVELOP YOUR OWN SENSE OF STYLE

Chances are, heaven will not carry any fashion magazines. So why worry about how you measure up to the latest trends here on earth? There's a lot of pressure from advertisers, society, and peers (regardless of whether you're seventeen or seventy) to look and dress a certain way. You know the rules . . . no white shoes after Labor Day. Don't mix plaids and stripes. "Just say no" to a mullet or a bouffant hairstyle. Diet until you can wear a bikini with pride. Discard anything with shoulder pads. Buy new clothes each and every season to make sure you remain "in style."

When God was here on earth, what did He choose to wear? From the Gospels, we can tell that Jesus stuck with the basic robe and sandals ensemble. Although He was—and still is—the King of kings, Jesus clothed Himself with the outfit common workers wore. It was utilitarian and durable. It wasn't designed to stand out in a crowd or call undue attention to Jesus' divinity. It simply covered His body and helped protect Him from the elements. Jesus' "style" reflected the character of His heart—that of a humble servant.

What's the character of your heart? Express it with your very own style. Be authentic. Be pure. Be creative. Be comfortable. As long as your clothes are within your budget and work well for whatever purpose God has set in front of you today, the cut and color are simply an outward expression of who you are. Don't dress for success—or to impress. Dress to express the unique individual God designed you to be. Then, forget about what you're wearing and put your focus back on who you're becoming. Let the real you shine through and through, from hairdo to shoes.

41

LISTEN
FOR GOD

People who say they "talk to God" are often regarded with more than a bit of skepticism. But the truth is that all people talk to God on occasion, whether they believe He's there or not. Universally, people cry out for help in desperate situations, even when they know no human ear can hear them. That's the innate call of their hearts, the default switch of automatic prayer that all humans are designed with to help guide them home to God's throne. Yes, people who talk to God are really quite common. However, those who listen to Him are not.

One reason is that God's voice isn't always easy to hear. Unless you're actively listening for Him, you may come to the conclusion that He is silent—or not even there at all. To better attune your ears to His whisper, become acquainted with His words in the Bible. The more familiar you are with His words, the easier you'll find it is to distinguish His voice from your own random thoughts. Also, get in the habit of listening for God's response when you speak to Him. Don't just ramble off a laundry list of what you want Him to do for you, slap on an "amen," and then go on to the next chore on your to-do list. Think about whom you are speaking to. Pray that what He wants would be done. Ask God to help you hear His voice more clearly. Then, sit quietly and listen for His response.

When you do feel His words of truth echo through your heart, when you believe He's whispering the direction in which He wants you to go or what alterations He wants you to make in your life, act on what you hear. You'll begin to see positive change taking place. On the other hand, if you are not seeing signs of improvement, you're obviously having a very one-sided conversation. But don't be discouraged. The more you listen for and respond to God's voice here on earth, the more acquainted you'll become with the sound of heaven.

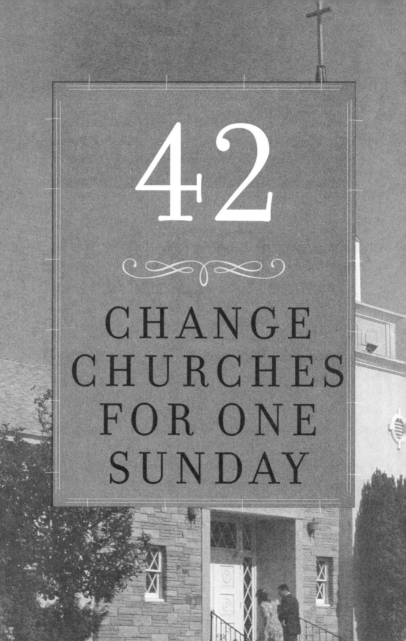

42

CHANGE
CHURCHES
FOR ONE
SUNDAY

Before you get to heaven, it's a good idea to get to know a few of your future neighbors. Not the ones you usually hang around with, but the ones who are different from you. The ones whose worship services are too contemporary or too traditional, too loud or too staid, too charismatic or not charismatic enough. These neighbors may live in a different part of town, dress in a different style, speak a different language, or have a different hue of epidermis than you do—but you're going to be worshiping side by side with them one day in heaven. And on that day, no one's going to be debating denominational differences.

Until that time, catch a glimpse of heaven by visiting a different church some Sunday. Choose one that is a different denomination from your own. Then, walk into the service with an open mind and an open heart. People may welcome you warmly—or not. How they respond to you is irrelevant. You are the one who is purposefully choosing to risk really living and loving before you go to heaven. Your example of spending one Sunday expanding the borders of your church "box" may encourage others to do the same.

Once you've arrived, join in the prayer and the praise. Listen closely to the pastor's words. Strike up a conversation with those around you before or after the service. Focus on what you have in common instead of on what sets you apart. Ask them how long they've gone to the church and why they're happy to call it home. Ask about their family, their lives, and their dreams. You may end up making a new friend in the process. You may also learn something new about God, worship, and the beauty of the place you'll someday call Home.

43

TAKE A
"LONG
CUT"

Efficiency and productivity can be aspects of a life well spent here on earth. But they don't tell the whole story. That's because "making the most of every moment" applies to more than what you do. It also plays a part in discovering who you are. At times, exploring the depth and breadth of life, uncovering your unique place in God's creation, and dwelling in the richness and possibility of it all can look a lot like wasting time.

It usually happens in unplanned moments, in the presence of beauty or the shadow of tragedy. Something slows you down, changes your plans, or shatters your heart. Suddenly, you're aware that there's so much more to life than what's jotted down in your weekly planner. Some things can't be measured, categorized, or even fully described in words. But they're real. And just getting close to them makes you want to savor life instead of simply utilizing the time you have in a proficient manner. But before you know it, you find yourself up and running again at warp speed, unaware of God's presence and the miracles He's woven into even the most average of days.

Before that happens yet again, choose to roll back the pace of your life. Eliminate a few nonessential commitments. Make time for wasting time. When your life has breathing room, you can choose a "long cut" home from work, simply because it's more scenic. You can prepare a home-cooked meal instead of picking up fast food yet again. On occasion, you can even sit and do nothing other than enjoy the feel of an afternoon breeze dancing across your face.

With the clamor of daily chaos better under control, you'll find you can hear God more clearly, enabling you to experience the wonder of life this side of heaven more fully. Your newfound pace can help welcome God's perfect peace into your life.

44

❧❦❧

BLESS AN
ENEMY

Think of the person you'd least like to see alongside you in heaven . . . perhaps someone who has hurt or betrayed you. Someone who has done the unthinkable. Someone who seems to have a personal vendetta against you for reasons you may not even know. Deep inside you, justice cries out, "This person deserves to be punished." Then mercy chimes in, "This person should be forgiven." All the while grace whispers softly, "What this person needs most is unconditional love."

That's exactly what God has extended to you. Unconditional love goes beyond forgiveness, although forgiveness is necessary to help love grow. Unconditional love chooses to treat an enemy the same way you would a friend, to bestow blessings in place of revenge. Unconditional love gives others a glimpse of heaven.

There are many practical ways you can "bless" an enemy with love. Praying regularly for those who have wronged you is a great way to begin. When you pray for someone, your view of that person changes to become more like God's. You begin to see needs in your former "enemy's" life that perhaps God can use you to help fill. Ask God for creativity and the opportunity to put your prayers into action. Ask Him to help you stop reliving the wrongs of the past through gossip. Changing the words you say can help change the way you think and feel.

Although choosing to bless an enemy obviously benefits that individual in this life, and perhaps even the next, it also benefits you. It releases you from feelings of bitterness and anger. It allows your forgiveness to go beyond sincere words toward healing damaged emotions. It helps set you free. The freer you are to love others— including those who seem unlovable—the more joyful your journey toward heaven will be.

45

CREATE A
SELF-
PORTRAIT

alling all artists!" If you have any doubt that this group includes you, consider this: You were created in God's image. You're a reflection of what He's like. If He's the most amazing artist of all time—and He is—then you must have at least a little artistic flair woven into you. So answer the call. Choose any medium you like. Find a pencil, a crayon, a box of children's watercolors, a ball of clay, or even a bank of freshly fallen snow. Then, fashion a likeness of yourself. Go ahead. Put the book down and do it now. This chapter will wait until you're finished.

Done? Take a critical look at your work. Don't judge whether it's "gallery worthy" or not. Just take a really good look at what you've done. Then ask yourself questions such as, *Why did I draw only a face?* or *Why did I choose to draw my whole body? Does anything in my artwork reveal my age? What "part" of my work am I most pleased with and why? Do I think I look handsome or pretty or plain? Did I choose to accentuate the features about myself that I like most—or least?"*

Then talk to the Master. Ask Him how He sees you and how His perspective compares with your own. Tell Him what you like, and dislike, about the way He made you. You can be honest. The fact is He already knows how you feel. Ask God to help you understand the roots of both the negative and the positive feelings you have about your physical self, to show you how His image is being reflected in you, and to work with you to align your impressions more with His own. Before you receive the new body God's promised to give you in heaven, it's good to appreciate the lovingly crafted one He's provided for you here and now.

46

❦

SELECT
A LIFE
VERSE

The Bible is filled with great verses. Lots of them. Verses that challenge you, convict you, encourage you, and ultimately draw you closer to the One you love. While being consistent in reading the whole of Scripture is important, applying what you learn is even more so. One way to do that is to take God's Word to heart. That means getting intimate with a portion of Scripture by studying it, memorizing it, turning it over in your mind, and putting what you learn into practice. It means weighing your life against God's truth.

Choosing a life verse helps you do just that. Think of it as a purpose statement for your life. A successful business knows what its primary purpose is, what it hopes will set it apart from every other business in town. Perhaps that purpose is to serve the best burrito in the county or offer the speediest pizza delivery downtown. What do you see as God's primary purpose for your life? It may be to love others as you love yourself, to proclaim God's message through every aspect of your life, or to serve God by serving others. It's true that God asks you to do all these things, but what one area does God want you to become an "expert" in? What characteristic does your heart cry out most deeply for? Mercy? Purity? Truth? Humility? Find a verse that captures your most heartfelt cry to God.

Finding that verse may take some time. As you read through the Bible, record every verse that summarizes the kind of person you want to be. Live with each verse for a while. Try it on for size. Think about it as you go through your day. Ask God to help you apply it in life-changing ways. After a while, you'll find one that strongly resonates with you. Use it as a flashlight during dark times, a scale to weigh who you are against who you long to be, and a promise of what God can do as you wholly lean on Him.

47

BE SILENT FOR ONE WHOLE DAY

There's an old adage that says, "Silence is golden." That's because there's great value in keeping your mouth shut now and then. Such as when you're getting ready to correct someone else's response. When you're about to join in on the latest gossip. When your emotions are about to spill over into unkind words. When you need to be quiet enough to hear God speak . . . and the list goes on.

By putting yourself on a verbal fast for a day, you'll discover that you do have the self-control it takes to keep your lips closed. But first, you have to make a commitment toward making this day happen. Choose a time when you don't have to go to work or have other scheduled commitments. Spend the day at a hotel, retreat center, or campsite. If that's not an option, ask those in your household to honor your time by not asking you questions or trying to strike up a conversation.

Begin your "quiet day" with silent prayer. You'll find as the day goes by that less external conversation opens the door to more internal conversation with both God and yourself. Read from the book of Proverbs, focusing on verses that deal with the tongue and all of the wicked, wily, and wonderful things it can do. Write down any proverbs that hit home and memorize the one you feel God most wants you to apply. Bring it to mind throughout the day. During the rest of your time, go about your day as usual. If you have to say something, try to stick with "yes," "no," or "thank you." Don't turn on the TV, stereo, or radio. Simply enjoy the quiet. Listen to what others are really saying. Listen to the everyday sounds of birds, the wind, or children laughing. Then, close your day by again talking to the One who speaks most clearly in silence. You may discover that silence is more than golden. It's a necessity, and you need to be more intentional about working it into your life.

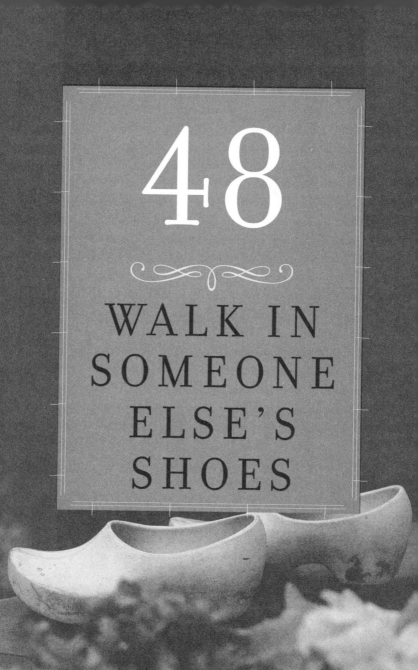

48

WALK IN SOMEONE ELSE'S SHOES

Okay, so you don't really have to walk like an Egyptian, but you do need to try to put yourself in his or her shoes. Actually, the shoes of anyone from another part of the globe will do. The key is to venture out of your familiar corner of the world and immerse yourself in a different culture for a while.

The ways to do this are limited only by the size of your imagination and scope of your sense of adventure. Take a class to learn the Thai language. Try an Ethiopian restaurant. Watch a Turkish dance troupe. Attend a local celebration of the Scottish games. Eat with chopsticks. Watch a foreign film with subtitles. Learn to play mahjongg. Dance an Argentine tango. Listen to Armenian folk songs. Study Greek history. Read a book translated from another language. Host a foreign exchange student. Open your home to a refugee from Sudan. Open your heart to a friend for whom English is a second language.

No matter what you choose to do, dare to step outside what's familiar. It's guaranteed to be more than just a learning experience. It's a way to diminish prejudice and expand empathy. It helps you better see people the way God does. God created people in a kaleidoscope of color, personality, and potential for social behaviors. Custom and culture are simply an expression of the wild buffet of human behavior. When you learn to enjoy the variety of cultures the world provides, instead of fearing them or weighing them against your own, you can look beyond them to what really matters—the heart of an individual who is precious to God. The more you learn to see people from the inside out, the more you'll learn to appreciate and love the individuals who may one day share your home in heaven.

49

❧∼❧

GET A
MASSAGE

I f you've indulged in a massage before, chances are no one needs to convince you that it was time well spent. However, if you've never had a massage, now's the perfect time to ask yourself why. For some people, the cost can be prohibitive. That's a perfectly valid reason to be content with a back rub from a friend or spouse. But if even that is something you shy away from, dig deeper into the "whys" of your hesitation before you head to heaven.

One reason people shun spa types of experiences is that they find it hard to accept a little pampering. They are perfectly happy serving others but feel guilty or overly indulgent spending time and money on themselves. Some people view this kind of attitude as a sign of humility. In actuality, it's often a sign of a person who has a hard time receiving with open arms.

All of God's gifts are free, unearned, and undeserved. God's gifts are born out of His love for you, out of His desire for you to enjoy good things. Enjoying a massage can be a time of worship as you thank God for all the ways, both big and small, that He adds joy, relaxation, and beauty to your life. It can be a time to clear your head and energize you toward accomplishing what God wants you to do in this life. It can be a time of physical and even emotional healing. It's your attitude, not simply the physical experience, that can help make having a massage such a meaningful activity.

Schedule a massage with a purpose in mind: Ask God to help you focus on the moment at hand. Ask Him to help you feel comfortable about your own body and fully enjoy the gifts He lavishes on you every day of your life. Ask Him to help you freely receive, as well as give. Then, lie down, relax, and enjoy.

50

MAKE
YOURSELF
AT HOME IN
A CEMETERY

In the movies, cemeteries are creepy places. They are not locales where you want to hang out or by any means make yourself at home. But, in reality, cemeteries are more like train stations than "final resting grounds." They are filled with the luggage people leave behind, the broken bodies they no longer want or need once they receive their tickets to paradise. Spending time in a cemetery can help prepare you for the day you will make that same journey.

You may choose to visit the gravesite of someone you are looking forward to seeing again in heaven. Or you may choose to stroll among the castoff luggage of strangers who may wind up as your eternal next-door neighbors. Wherever you choose to go, go with a prayer-filled heart. Your own mortality is not something to be taken lightly. Psalm 116:15 says, "Precious in the sight of the LORD is the death of his saints." You became His saint the day you chose to follow Him, to accept His gift of eternal life. Your life here on earth is important to you, God, and those you love. But it isn't the end.

As you wander through the gravestones, contemplate what awaits you down the road. Consider the length of eternity and what God has revealed about heaven. There, you'll meet God face-to-face. You'll receive a new body. You'll enjoy a new heaven and a new earth. There'll be angels and worship and beauty. Sorrow will be a thing of the past. There will be no more good-byes. Allow what you know of heaven to make a difference in your life here and now. Live with one foot on earth and the other poised in midstep toward your future home. Anticipate your journey with joy, while making the most of each day God has set aside for you to live here on earth.

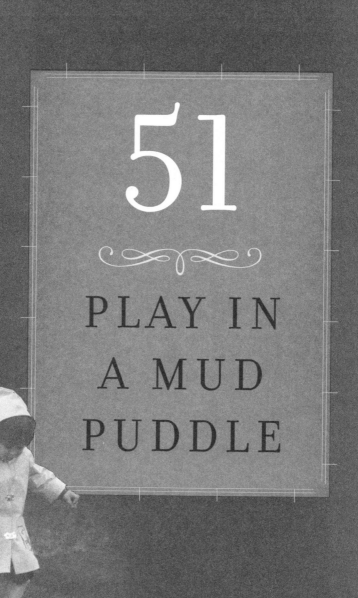

51

PLAY IN
A MUD
PUDDLE

God never said, "Cleanliness is next to godliness." In fact, you won't find that often-repeated proverb anywhere in the Bible. Cleanliness may be hygienic, desirable, and the socially acceptable norm, but sometimes it's good to go all out and get down-right dirty. If you have any doubt, make a play date with a mud puddle.

All you need is a steady rainstorm and a patch of good, old-fashioned dirt. Then, invite some small children, spontaneous teen-agers, or adventurous adults to join in the fun. When it comes to cast-ing off convention and rediscovering a bit of childlike joy, the more the merrier. Once you've gathered the "dirty dozen" together (give or take five or ten), simply plop yourself down in the middle of the biggest puddle you can find and invite your guests to do the same. Make mud pies. Give mud facials. Roll, shimmy, and scoot. Let the mud slip through your fingers and squish between your toes. Giggles and groans are sure to follow.

After you're thoroughly soaked and soiled, make the trek back home. Have a pile of old towels waiting for you by the door. If it's warm enough, you might want to hose off before going inside to shower. (For some people, cleaning up may be even more fun than getting dirty!) After putting your muddy clothes into the washer, invite your guests to get together and enjoy snacks and chat. No doubt the conversation will be an interesting one after such a unique experience.

There's nothing wrong with making a mess now and then—or even looking like one. And since it is unlikely that there will be any mud in heaven, you'll want to be sure to frolic in the puddles here on earth while you have the chance. Then you may be less hesitant to take the next opportunity that could leave you hot, sweaty, dirty, or disheveled. Who knows? That opportunity may be one that God has been anxiously waiting to bring your way.

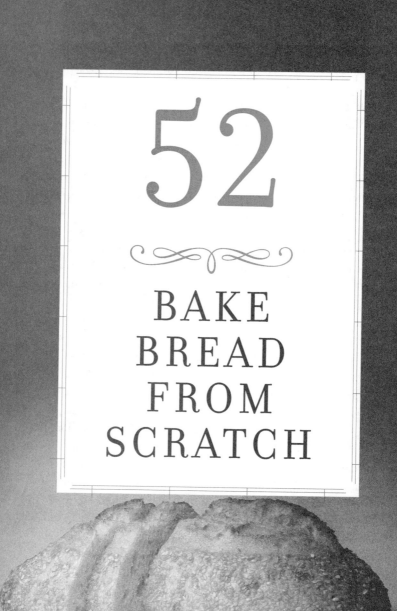

52

BAKE
BREAD
FROM
SCRATCH

H ere's something that sounds like a waste of time and energy. Instead of going to the grocery store, visiting your favorite bakery, or using your own handy-dandy bread maker, make a loaf of bread from scratch. Not a box, not a mix, not frozen dough, quick bread, or carrot muffins. Make an honest-to-goodness yeasty batch of sticky dough. Knead it. Let it rise. Then, bake it until it's golden brown.

Why, you might ask, should you go to all the trouble? After all, the task not only promises to be time-consuming and dirty-dish inducing, it doesn't even save you money. However, the truth is that when you make a loaf of bread, your level of gratitude has a chance to rise along with the dough. While you're mixing and measuring, consider how much it took just to get that flour to your mixing bowl. Grain had to be planted, watered, harvested, ground, packaged, and delivered to market. Consider how many people it took to get that flour into your hands—as well as all those who help bring clean water to your tap, and electricity or gas to your stove, created the loaf pan you're baking in, and even crafted the knife you use to cut the finished product. Soon you realize that having the ingredients and tools to make a simple sandwich involves a major group effort.

If this is your first loaf of homemade bread, success isn't guaranteed. Getting the yeast to rise correctly can be tricky business. (Yet another reason to be grateful for all those who bake bread for you!) But whether your bread rises or falls, browns or burns, cut yourself a slice after it cools. Sit down and eat it with God. Thank Him for the gift He's given you of community, even with those you may never meet. Thank Him for His daily provision. Ask Him to help you be heartfelt and sincere before every meal when you ask His blessing on your daily bread.

53

~~~~~~

EXPLORE
YOUR
FAMILY
TREE

Genealogy is important to God. If you have any doubt, check out the lists of who begat whom sprinkled throughout the Old Testament. For that matter, check out the beginning of the first book of the New Testament. Matthew opens with the genealogy of Jesus. Apparently, not even Immaculate Conception can circumvent someone from being intertwined within the branches of a family tree.

Jesus' earthly lineage is littered with saints and sinners, those who followed God and those who ran in the other direction. Every individual had his or her own unique chapter to add to the history of the world and the heritage of Christ. How familiar are you with the chapters your predecessors have written? Chatting with elderly relatives, perusing old scrapbooks, and even doing a little digging on the Internet can help you get a better picture of where you've come from.

As to where you're going, every branch on your family tree has a story to tell and lessons to learn. It's been said that those who don't learn from history are doomed to repeat it. Contemplate both the strengths and weaknesses of your family line. Every individual has a God-given destiny to fill. Whether your relatives produced the good fruit God intended them to bear depends on how they responded to the One who planted them in the first place.

But that's only the beginning of your story. . . . You have a spiritual family tree as well as an earthly one. You have a Father in heaven who is perfect and holy, whose lineage of loving you stretches back to the dawn of time. You also have brothers and sisters bound to you through the bloodline of faith. So feel free to explore your family tree. Climb into its branches. Survey its roots. Sample its fruit. The more you know, the more God can help you grow.

54

BREAK A LONGTIME HABIT

I t's something that gets in the way . . . of your health, of your dreams, of your ability to feel good about yourself. You know what it is. That pesky habit that's been hanging around for as long as you can remember. It could be as innocuous as biting your nails or as insidious as visiting Internet sites you'd be ashamed to view if others were in the room. Whatever it is, don't try to drag it along with you all the way to heaven. Kick that habit right out of your life.

You may say, "But I've tried and I can't." That was then and this is now. Today is a new day, a new opportunity for victory. God is right beside you, cheering for you, strengthening you, convicting you of how this habit of yours is robbing you of true freedom and joy. If your habit has such a strong hold on your life that it's become an addiction, find professional help. If you're afraid that by admitting you have a problem others will find out your "dark secret," rest assured that if they haven't suspected it already, time will assuredly bring it to light. God cares too much for you to have it any other way.

Be courageous enough to look beyond your habit to the reason why you started it in the first place. What were you searching for? Comfort? Excitement? Acceptance? Escape? Whatever hole you were trying to fill in your life, God can fill it to overflowing in a positive, productive way that brings freedom instead of bondage. Facing your weakness and your deepest needs isn't easy. It will take time, perseverance, and humility. But you, and the abundant life God longs for you to live, are worth the effort. Why wait another day? Begin to break that habit before it breaks you.

55

REKINDLE ROMANCE

Love is a feeling, but it's also so much more. It's a commitment to reach out, even when the feeling isn't there at the moment. If you're married or dating, you know through experience that romance can be a wonderful part of a loving relationship. But you also know that some seasons of life seem to hold a little more romance than others. Whatever season you're in right now, today is the perfect time to rekindle the romance of early courtship and reconnect on a more intimate level.

Before you take action, take some time to think about . . . What first attracted you to the one you love? What was the most romantic time you have ever had together? What made it that way? What is your idea of a perfect romantic evening? How does it differ from that of your spouse or boyfriend or girlfriend?

After giving these questions some serious thought and prayer, it's time to come up with a plan. Though spontaneous romance is wonderful, a well-planned romantic interlude can actually help put more spontaneity back into your relationship.

Habit and complacency are romance killers, so shake things up a little. Eat dinner on a blanket in front of the fireplace. Take the kids to a sitter's before he or she comes home from work. Send him or her flowers—without an occasion. Write "I ♥ U" in the steam on the bathroom mirror or in whipped cream on a piece of pie. Do what the other person would enjoy most, instead of trying to fulfill your own romantic fantasies.

Most of all, speak lovingly to, and about, each other. Your words reveal what your heart is really like. Be honest. Be open. Lavish praise on your significant other and don't take each other for granted. You may find that your loving "feelings" are no longer buried but rather are bursting into full bloom.

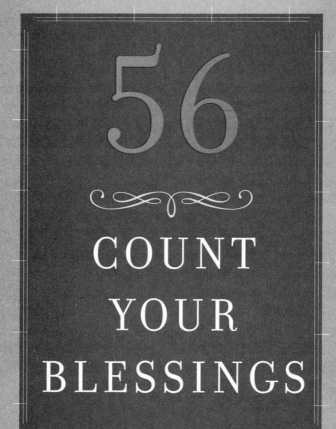

56

COUNT
YOUR
BLESSINGS

Count your blessings" is a phrase so overused and undercontemplated that it's lost much of its true meaning. But the truth is, the gifts you've received from God are beyond measure. Trying to count them, or even take note of them, is certain to have a positive impact on you. It will fill your heart with gratitude and praise.

You can start this very minute and continue on throughout eternity. Take a moment to consider the blessing of your body—such as your beating heart, pumping blood, and exhaling-inhaling lungs. Look around you. Thank God for the possessions you own and the finances He provides to help you pay for your basic needs. Picture the faces of those you love. Praise God for the unique person He has made each one of them. Continue by considering blessings such as God's gift of the Bible, His promise of heaven, His unfailing love. Then recall all the little things God does every day to bring joy and purpose to your life. Your personal list could go on and on.

To make counting your blessings a regular part of your life, begin a blessings book. Take a few moments every morning or evening to write down what you want to thank God for that day. Every Thanksgiving, sit down and read through what you've written over the past year. Set aside some time that day to do something other than stuff the turkey, eat pumpkin pie, and wash dishes. Set a date with God to thank Him for how He has blessed you over the past year. The more things you find to thank Him for, the more open your eyes and heart will be to see even more blessings that you may have missed in the past—and the more you'll realize how deeply you are loved.

57

LET MUSIC MOVE YOU

M usic is a language that reaches beyond words. Its message of joy or sadness, majesty or tyranny, courage or fear, crosses the barriers of language, culture, and time. A simple musical scale in the hands of a talented musician can yield endless melodies to entertain, soothe, excite, or astound a crowd—or praise God in a unique way. Music has been part of the human expression since the dawn of time. And since the Bible reveals it is also part of the culture of heaven, that means God is no stranger to notes and rests, arpeggios and arias. Undoubtedly, He was the very first maestro, the One who created the magic of music before man ever hummed his very first tune.

Since there is so much of the divine intertwined in the mystery of music, it's important to spend some time really listening to it before you go to heaven. Instead of simply turning on the radio during the morning commute or putting on a CD during dinnertime, give your full attention to a piece of your favorite music. Put on an instrumental CD, so words won't get in the way of the music itself. Lie down with your eyes closed. (Or better yet, go to a live performance of the symphony.) Focus on the melody. Then, concentrate on the harmonies. Try to pick out one instrument at a time and listen to the individual music lines that are combining to create the finished piece. Try to decipher what the composer was trying to say. At the same time ask, *What's God trying to say to me?*

Music can stir emotions in a profound way. Let it. Ask God to reveal Himself through what you hear, to speak to you in a way that only music can. If you play an instrument, compose a melody that expresses how you feel about God's love for you. Let music, whether it's your own or composed by someone else, move you closer to Him.

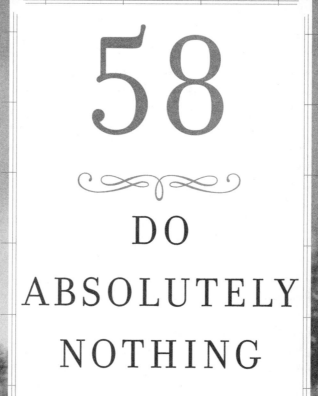

58

DO
ABSOLUTELY
NOTHING

Doing nothing is actually doing something. It is giving yourself permission to sit, relax, and just be. Guilt free. After all, God's design for you is to be a human being, not a human doing. However, trying to make every day count in this life can easily be confused with filling every waking moment to the brim with activity. But look at God's example. After a busy six days of creating, He took a day off to relax and enjoy what He'd accomplished. Jesus encouraged the disciples to go away with Him to a quiet place and rest when life got too hectic. If God, who has all of creation in His care, can take time to relax, certainly you can too.

Planning how to do nothing sounds a little counterproductive, but if you've grown accustomed to life in the fast lane, your psyche may need a refresher course. Take a lesson from your childhood. Lie on the lawn and watch the clouds go by. Sit on a park bench and listen for a bird symphony. Hold the hand of someone you love, just because. Float on your back in a lake with your eyes closed. Pet a sleeping kitten. Sit cross-legged on the sidewalk and watch the ants march by. Take a nap, just because you're sleepy.

Watching TV, listening to music, or tinkering with household projects that are on your to-do list doesn't count as "nothing." Your brain needs some time to clear out the noise and the clutter of your everyday life, so you can hear God's voice and your own thoughts and questions about life more clearly. You need time to be still, inside and out. Whether you choose to take five minutes, an afternoon, or a whole day to do nothing, let go of your worries and plans for tomorrow. Hand each one of them to God. Then, sit back and enjoy just being yourself.

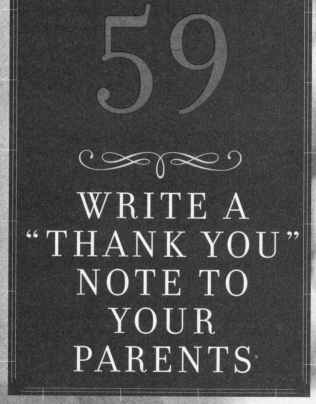

59

WRITE A "THANK YOU" NOTE TO YOUR PARENTS

Parenting is a tough job. Some moms and dads do it well—balancing love, sacrifice, and joy along with wisdom, discipline, and grace. Others, for a variety of reasons, struggle to maintain their balance on the parental tightrope. Still others are so busy trying to parent themselves that they abandon their kids physically or emotionally. Whatever category your parents fall into, you're in their debt. God used them to give you life and fashion your character in this world. God asks you to do something for them in return. He asks you to honor them.

Honoring your parents, especially once you're an adult, can also feel like a tightrope walk at times. But it's a journey God has asked you to take, regardless of your past or present circumstances. Honor isn't something your parents earn. It's a free gift you extend to them without asking for anything in return. It's a gift God can help you offer over and over again through your words and actions—and at times through your forgiveness. One gift you should honor your parents with before you get to heaven is a word of thanks for all they've done.

It doesn't matter whether your parents are living in this world or the next. What matters is that you spend some time considering how your parents have helped you become who you are today. Give your gratitude permanence by putting it into words. Write down what your parents did right. Mention the things you admire most about them, what they've taught you, what they sacrificed for you, the support they provided—physically, financially, and emotionally. If possible, send the letter to them. If not, read it aloud to God. As your only perfect Parent, God knows both your story and theirs. As you honor your parents, at the same time you'll be honoring Him.

60

WALK IN A
REDWOOD
GROVE

S tep onto the cinnamon-colored forest floor. Layers of shed redwood bark blanket the ground, muting the sound of your footsteps to a whisper befitting of what feels like a living sanctuary. Dappled sunlight filters through branches that tower up to 350 feet high, rivaling the stained glass of the finest Gothic cathedrals. Welcome to a grove of giant sequoias.

Sequoias are the largest living things on earth . . . measuring three times taller than the length of a blue whale, weighing more than eighty elephants, living up to two thousand years. But under the forest floor, redwoods tell a surprisingly different story. Their roots grow only six to ten feet deep. The secret to surviving two centuries of raging rains and winds lies in the fact that redwoods don't go it alone. They grow together in groves, intertwining their roots for strength and stability.

Walking through a redwood forest affords an awesome look at the majesty of God's creation. At the same time, it teaches a silent lesson on the importance of community. Having a "grove" of people around you who will be there when the storms of life blow in, who'll encourage you to grow right along with them, and for whom you can return the favor, will help keep you strong and stable. There are lots of ways you can intertwine your life with others. Get to know your neighbors. Involve yourself with a local church community. Speak words of encouragement and hope. Be a shoulder to cry on, while letting others help dry your own tears.

The majority of the world's redwoods grow along Northern California's Pacific coast. Several groves in this area make up an official World Heritage Site. Before you go to heaven, take a walk among these giants. Bask in their beauty. Find calm in the quiet. Let them teach you how to stand tall by leaning on others and intertwining your life with theirs.

61

SWING!

Think back to when you were a kid. Remember the joy of visiting a new playground?

Here was your chance to swing, slide, climb, hang, and teeter-totter the day away. It was active. It was imaginative. And it was downright fun. For adults, physical activity usually falls into two categories: competition or exercise. Although it may be considered recreation, adult "play" often loses touch with the simple joy of using your body to run, jump, reach, and roll.

Reconnect with your inner gymnast by visiting a playground near you. Your best bet is to take a couple of kids along . . . your own kids, grandkids, neighborhood kids, or simply kids you know who could use a friend. Allow them to be your teachers for the day. Ask them to show you how to use everything from the swings to the jungle gym. Let them be the experts. Listen carefully. Ask questions. (Their explanations and demonstrations alone will be worth the trip.) Then, try to do what they do.

Your body may not work quite as well as it did "back in the day." You may come home with a few sore muscles—or even find yourself in need of a Band-Aid or two. But don't let that stop you from getting out there and really playing. Try not to think of how many calories you're burning or compare the distance of your jump off the swing with that of the six-year-old swinging next to you. Leave your inhibitions and agendas behind and rediscover the joy of play. Who knows? Heaven may be filled with play days, times when you can try out your new body and simply enjoy the gift of movement. But until then, praise God for the body you have right now and for the kid inside who can still enjoy a good swing now and then.

62

READ THE
BIOGRAPHY
OF SOMEONE
YOU ADMIRE

I
f you wander among the shelves of the library or your favorite bookstore, you'll discover some truly amazing life stories in print. Some of the subjects will be familiar. Others' names may be downright famous. But among the stacks you'll also find biographies of those who have lived their lives in relative obscurity. Ordinary people who have overcome tremendous odds or accomplished remarkable feats—people whose everyday lives rival the best fiction on the market. Every biography on those shelves has a lesson to teach—some by example, others by way of a warning. Since your life is too short to learn all these lessons through personal experience, it makes good sense to learn from the experience of others.

Pick up a biography of someone whose life you've admired from afar. If you can't think of anyone who fits that bill, peruse the bookshelves. Read a few jacket covers. Ask friends about any biographies they've read that inspired them. Lean toward autobiographies over "unauthorized biographies," since it's best to hear a story from the one who has actually lived it firsthand. Then, sit down, open the book, and become acquainted with your new mentor. As you read, evaluate what you admire about this person. See if what you admire changes after you've finished the book. Ask yourself what you would have done differently if you had been in his or her shoes. See if there are any lessons you've learned that you can apply to your own life.

Don't forget to ask yourself what God would think of this person's life choices. If you find yourself admiring people God would not admire, take time to talk to God about your reasons. See what He has to say in light of that person's eternal story. If you need to get better insight into God's way of thinking, why not read His biography? The Bible.

63

ATTEND A
GALLERY
OPENING

You may feel right at home attending an artist's opening at a gallery. You may enjoy contemplating the artwork while munching miniscule snacks accompanied by artsy banter. Or you may feel like a fish out of water, flopping uncomfortably on an unknown yuppie shore. The point of attending the debut of an artist's collection is not to make your mark on the society circuit. It's to become more aware of the deeply personal connection between an artist and his or her creation.

Take the leap into an artist's world. Study each piece in the collection. Look for recurring themes or colors. Consider where the artist's greatest skill, and interest, lies. Pretend that money is no object and mentally choose your favorite piece. If you don't care for any piece in the collection, ask yourself why. Try to figure out what the artist is trying to express. Read any literature provided about the artist's experience, vision, and chosen medium. If you have the chance to meet the artist personally, which is one advantage of attending an opening rather than simply wandering into the gallery during regular business hours, take advantage of it. Ask the artist which piece is his or her favorite and why. Ask how long it took to create. Try to discover what fuels the artist's passion for this particular type of expression.

In the same way that an artist's work reveals a lot about who that person is, God's creation reveals a lot about His unchanging character, passion, and creativity. His gallery surrounds you and is open twenty-four hours a day. As you walk through it during your time here on earth, keep your eyes open. Each new dawn is a gallery opening. Each new day, a chance to discover more about the heart of the Artist who created the masterpiece you are.

64

REFUSE
TO ACT
YOUR AGE

Your age is just a number. It's a label to help you keep track of time. It's as indiscriminate as the days of the week. Wednesday may come after Tuesday, but does that make Wednesday any less valuable? It's true that your age can act as a kind of warning system, like a ten-minute buzzer reminding players that the end of a game is near. But it's just a reminder that every day takes you one step closer toward heaven. It's a cue to make the most of the days that lie ahead.

So don't let the age on your driver's license muffle the sound of your heart as it whispers, "Go for it." If you love having long hair, wear it that way, even after your braids go gray. Sign up for that parachute jump you've always dreamed of, even if you have to wear Depends. Strike up conversations with those who are young, old, and everything in between—choosing to focus on their value and God-given potential, instead of their age. Trade in the words *elderly* and *dignified* for words such as *authentic, unique,* and *still growing.* You can be mature and still experience every day of your life with childlike excitement and spontaneity. Actually, it's a sign of maturity and gratitude to God to do just that.

Focus more on the benefits of getting older than on the difficulties. Cherish the wisdom, discipline, and great memories that can be gained only through living long and well. Recognize the treasure of a friendship or marriage that spans decades. Rest in the comfort of knowing that God will see you through the hard times just as He has always done in the past. Don't let a number bring you down. Let it spur you on toward making the most of every moment that lies between you and heaven.

65

PUSH
YOURSELF
TO THE
LIMIT

Running a marathon takes more than endurance and a good pair of shoes. It requires an attitude that says, "I haven't reached my limit. I know I can go farther than I've gone in the past." Some people seem to have been blessed with this attitude at birth. Others need to make a conscious decision to push themselves beyond their comfort zone. Whichever group you fall into is irrelevant. The important thing is that you won't know your true limits until you put them to the test.

Consider your current physical, mental, and spiritual limits. What is the most challenging thing you have ever undertaken and successfully achieved in each of these areas? Next, consider a goal that seems out of reach in each area but is one you'd really like to accomplish. It could be running a real marathon—or simply jogging around the block. Maybe it's learning to speak a different language or play the piano. Perhaps it's volunteering to lead a small group at church or consistently spending fifteen minutes each day reading the Bible and talking to God. Your current limits, and how far you decide to push them, are between you and God. This is not a competition. It's an expedition, a journey that will lead you farther into the all-too-often-undiscovered territory of your God-given potential.

Pushing yourself beyond what comes naturally forces you to rely more on God and less on your own strengths. It also helps you become more strategic and disciplined. This may sound as if life will resemble a military boot camp. Nothing is farther from the truth. Increasing your ability to stay focused and persevere toward a goal, especially one that's difficult to reach, actually allows you to relax and enjoy life at a deeper level. It frees you up to better use time and abilities that once may have gone to waste. It helps you get more out of this life before you move on to the next.

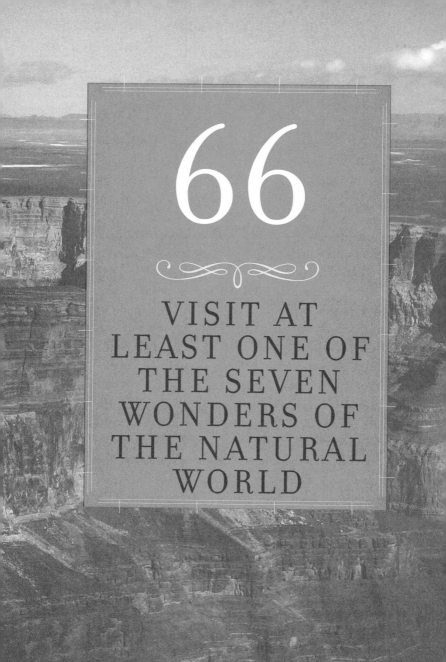

66

VISIT AT
LEAST ONE OF
THE SEVEN
WONDERS OF
THE NATURAL
WORLD

The world is filled with wonders, but some receive more notoriety than others. Whatever is bigger, bolder, or most outrageous gets people talking—and those who hear their stories end up wanting to see firsthand what all the fuss is about. When it comes to the Seven Wonders of the World, the simple fact that people from all over the globe continue to be drawn to these sites—and amazed—should be enough of a reason for you to long to experience at least one of them yourself.

Of the Seven Wonders of the World, only the Pyramids of Giza in Egypt remain—if you don't count the pieces of the Mausoleum of Halicarnassus that are housed in the British Museum. The other five awe-inspiring colossal creations of man fell to earthquake, fire, or marauding armies. However, the Seven Wonders of the Natural World—God's Original Seven Wonders—are still very much intact and awaiting your arrival. If you travel to Australia or Arizona, you can even enjoy a twofer: Ayers Rock and the Great Barrier Reef are situated Down Under, while the Grand Canyon and the Barringer Meteor Crater are within a few hours of each other in northern Arizona. The remaining wonders can be found in Switzerland (the Matterhorn), Africa (Victoria Falls), and the border of Tibet and Nepal (Mount Everest).

Visiting anything that evokes wonder presents a perfect opportunity to have a chat with God. Consider what it is that leaves you awestruck. Chat with Him about what amazes you, surprises you, or fills you with such a sense of beauty, mystery, or majesty—what reminds you most of Him. You may even want to come up with your own personal list of God's Seven Wonders of the World, listing the top seven places you've visited that have brought an invisible God most clearly into view for you. Then, share your list with others. You may inspire them to make a trip to see what all the fuss is about.

67

FASTEN YOUR SEAT BELT

Your final destination is secure. However, you do have some control over whether the journey you'll take to get there will be bumpy or smooth. The difference depends on the choices you make every day. Not every choice is a clear-cut right or wrong. Some choices are simply wise or unwise. Being wise about the choices you make concerning the care of your body, mind, and spirit will affect the "road conditions" of your life.

Though you are in God's care, you also have a responsibility to care for yourself. When it comes to your body, you know the basics: Fasten your seat belt. Wear sunscreen. Watch your weight. Don't drink and drive. Exercise. Get enough sleep. Have regular checkups. It's not that taking care of your body is difficult, but it is something that needs ongoing attention. Your body is amazingly complex and its parts are interdependent. Neglecting one area of preventative health care or personal safety can have consequences that affect the overall well-being of your entire body, and therefore your life.

The same goes for your mind and spirit. Make choices that draw you closer to God instead of those that push you away from Him. Fill your mind with good things—things that are wholesome, honorable, and beautiful. Carefully select the movies you watch and the books you read. If anxiety or depression begins to pull your mind in unhealthy directions, get some help from a physician or mental health professional. Keep your spirit healthy by wisely choosing to spend time with your loving heavenly Father. Ponder and apply what you read in the Bible. Develop spiritual support and a spirit of community by becoming involved in a local church. Every choice you make as to the care or neglect of your body, mind, and spirit has a consequence. Paving that road with positive consequences will assure you a smoother and more enjoyable journey to your final destination.

68

MAKE
YOUR
HOUSE A
HOME

Whether you're living in a starter home, an apartment, your parents' basement, a mansion, or a double-wide, your current address can be more than just the place where you reside. It can be your haven, your castle, and your "home, sweet home"—until you make the final move to your true home in heaven.

That's because a "dream home" here on earth isn't determined by its square footage, eye-catching appeal, or even by the length of time you reside in it. It's created moment by moment by the memories you make within its walls. Extending God's love to each person who comes through the door—whether it's a member of your family or a plumber fixing a leaky pipe—is crucial when it comes to making memories worth cherishing. Naturally, this also extends to any houseguests you may have. Love them with your actions, as well as your words. Make them comfortable by keeping things neat and clean, but don't work yourself to a frazzle trying to impress them with perfection in your housekeeping or culinary skills. Just be yourself. If you love to cook, feed guests something you feel at ease preparing. If you hate to cook, order pizza. Love makes any meal a feast.

As for decorating, a house feels more like a home when it reflects the personalities of the people who live in it. It may be tempting to try to recreate a scene from a magazine, but a real home never sends the message "Look, but don't touch." It invites others to sit on the furniture, grab a snack from the fridge, and kick off their shoes. Consider what you can do to help make your house more of a home. Every day is the perfect time to make a memory.

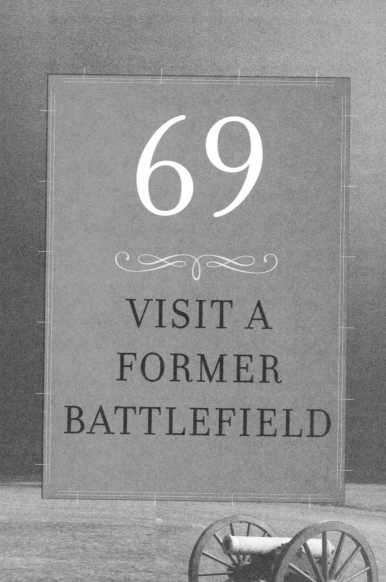

69

VISIT A
FORMER
BATTLEFIELD

Often it looks like nothing more than a grassy field dotted with a few trees or perhaps a rusty cannon or crumbling stronghold. You may find a plaque noting a date, a quote, and a fact or two about what transpired on that spot. On occasion, there may be a monument—or a gift shop. But no matter what "amenities" a former battlefield may hold, it's worth a stop and some time in thought.

Whether you happen to be passing by on a road trip or have chosen one as your destination, visiting a former battlefield is an important journey to take not only physically, but also mentally, emotionally, and spiritually. Once you arrive, take a moment to compare the peace of the present moment to what you imagine it might have been like during the heat of battle. Picture individuals just like yourself with families, dreams, and fears. Talk to God about freedom, sacrifice, and how privileged you are to enjoy the benefits of both. Take time to reflect on the fact that this very spot was the last place some people saw before they entered the gates of heaven.

Gettysburg, Wounded Knee, Pearl Harbor, the coast of Normandy, Ground Zero in New York, a former concentration camp in Germany, or the site of the Oklahoma City bombing are all destinations that can help you gain a better sense of the never-ending battle between good and evil, love and hate, idealism and truth. Some locations may fit the classic definition of "battlefield" better than others, but life-and-death battles need not fit into a strictly military mold. Every battle that is fought and every sacrifice that is made is worthy of recognition and remembrance.

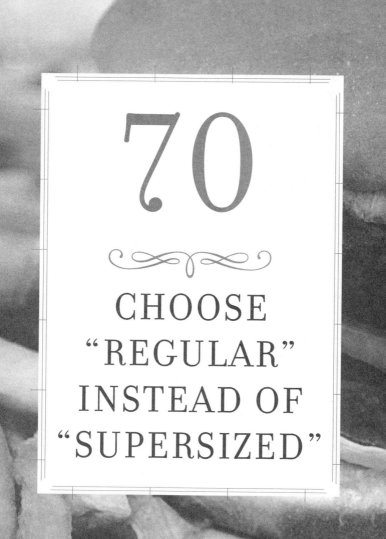

70

CHOOSE "REGULAR" INSTEAD OF "SUPERSIZED"

Just because something is supersized doesn't mean it's automatically a super choice. If you eat slowly and pay attention to how you're feeling, eating a regular-sized meal at your favorite fast-food restaurant can actually be more enjoyable than stuffing in those extra fries just because "more" sounds like the better deal. The difference between regular and supersized may be only forty cents, but it still means you're forty cents richer if you don't let your greed get the best of you.

Greed sounds like a pretty harsh word, but that's exactly what's behind the pull toward "bigger is better." Fast food isn't the only temptation. There's the pull to buy not simply a new car, but one with all the bells and whistles on it. Just because you happen to like hedgehogs, there's that tug to purchase everything you see that has a hedgehog likeness attached to it—and to continue collecting more and more. There's the draw to go for that job with the bigger salary, not because you need it or even because the job is something you're better suited to do, but because you feel better when you have "more" at your disposal.

An abundant life is not synonymous with an overflowing garage or expanding waistline. It isn't found in an abundance of things or thrills or accomplishments. Upgrading, upscaling, or being upwardly mobile cannot lead you there either. Only God can. The "more" He provides is more peace, more joy, and more contentment in this life. He supersizes your life by enabling you to make a greater impact on the world. When your life and thoughts are filled with God, you'll discover there isn't as much room for all of that other stuff that once seemed so important. You'll find your "less" beginning to feel a lot like "more."

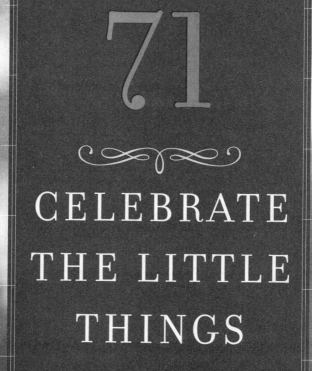

71

CELEBRATE
THE LITTLE
THINGS

Celebrations are landmarks on the road to heaven. They commemorate important events such as birthdays, weddings, anniversaries, and homecomings. But so much more in life deserves to be celebrated, so many little things that make a big difference in your everyday experience—the beauty of a sunset that stops you in your tracks; the first snowflake of the season; the first time you use the gym membership you purchased a year ago; the moment your child first says, "I love you"; the day you pay off a long-held debt.

Anything God brings your way that fills you with a special burst of joy is worthy of both thanks and celebration. That doesn't mean that every time a flower blooms you need to bring out the balloons and invite the neighbors over for cake. (Unless you want to!) Celebrations can be as simple as the delights they honor. Some can be as effortless as taking a moment out to thank God for what He's done. For others, you may want to light a candle at the dinner table and share with the family how God surprised you with joy today. Or perhaps you could take a photo commemorating a special moment and add it to a "simple celebrations" scrapbook. You could write a poem, song, or prayer. You could do something special for God, such as making a donation to those in need, since He's done something so special for you. Your gift may give someone else a cause for celebration!

No matter what you do, don't let the little joys of life pass you by. Find new and creative ways to commemorate and celebrate them. Heaven is bound to be filled with the spirit of celebration. Better start getting into the party mood here and now.

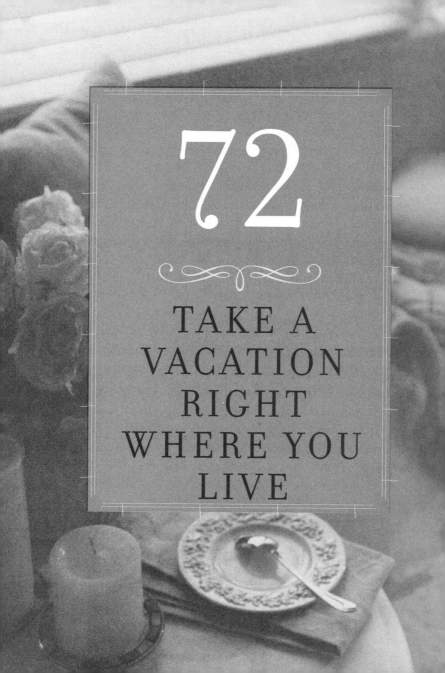

72

TAKE A VACATION RIGHT WHERE YOU LIVE

Vacation days are few and far between, so spending them wisely is, well, wise. While traveling out of town seems to embody the spirit of "getting away from it all," finances, family commitments, and even the stress of travel can pressure you to spend your vacation time in the same spot where you spend the rest of the year—at home. But time off at home doesn't have to be an oxymoron, nor does it have to feel like settling for second best. As a matter of fact, you can choose to vacation right where you live and enjoy a vacation that's worthy of the title "best ever." All it takes is a little planning and imagination.

Most stay-at-home vacations wind up being synonymous with "time to fix all the stuff I've ignored all year long." While crossing things off your to-do list is a worthy goal, the reality is, it's not a vacation. You need downtime. Time to rejuvenate. Play. Explore. Sleep in. Reconnect with family and friends. You need time to refresh your sense of joy in the life that God's given you. If you must get some projects accomplished, schedule one or two days to complete them. Work hard on those days and rest hard for the remainder of your time.

A few weeks before your vacation begins, take a close look at your local paper. Search for any community events that may coincide with your time off. Pick up literature from your chamber of commerce or bureau of tourism. Get to know every nook and cranny of your region. Take day trips to nearby parks or attractions. But don't forget to spend some time at home enjoying the special "spot" that God's given you in this world. Read a book from cover to cover. Watch your favorite movie again. Barbecue. Picnic. Nap. Laugh. Chat. Rediscover the truth that Dorothy from *The Wizard of Oz* knew all along: "There's no place like home. There's no place like home . . . "

73

BE AN
ANSWER
TO PRAYER

Pray for me." It is doubtful that you will hear these words in heaven, since all needs will be met there. But until then, it is likely that you will be asked to pray for someone you know. At times the words are spoken more in jest than as a personal request. But they can also be a heartfelt plea from those who are facing something that they know is too big for them to handle alone. Some of these people are already fervently praying on their own, but they know the power of joining together with others to pray for a common request. Still others may look to you as a "spiritual person," someone who has an "in" with God, which they feel they lack. Regardless of the whys behind the request, saying you'll pray for someone is making a commitment. The first way you can be an answer to prayer is by actually doing what you've promised.

The best way to keep your promise is to ask, "Would you like to pray together right now?" The Bible says that Christ is right there, praying alongside you, when two or more pray together in His name. Praying together is also a wonderful way to help those who are hesitant to begin conversing with God on their own. If taking a few moments to pray together is not an option, talk to God about the request at your first opportunity. There is less chance then that you'll forget to pray about it later. You may also want to write prayer requests in a journal at home—both your requests and those you've agreed to pray about for others. Refer to the journal during your times alone with God as a reminder of what to pray for, as well as what to praise Him for as you see His answers take shape.

Remember as you pray that God may want you to be an integral part of His answer. When He prompts you to fill a need, comfort a broken heart, or stand up for what is right, prayer is not enough. Action is the answer.

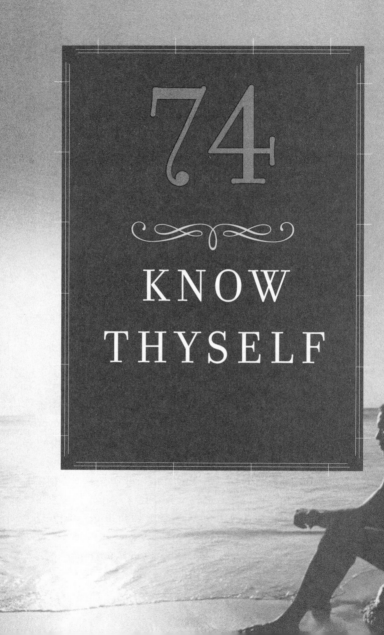

74

KNOW THYSELF

Y ou are here" are three of the most important words you can find on a map of unfamiliar territory. Even if the words themselves aren't actually printed there for you, your location better be firmly imprinted in your mind. If you don't know where you are, how can you get where you want to go?

On the road to heaven, knowing where you are means more than knowing your geographical location. It means knowing yourself. Knowing where you are physically, emotionally, mentally, relationally, and spiritually. Having a firm grasp on your own strengths and weaknesses. Understanding what gifts you have to offer and what talents need a little nurturing. Without knowing who you are right now, you cannot see how far you have to go to become the person God created you to mature into.

Sometimes it can be difficult to get a clear picture of who you are on your own. Your best resource is to go straight to God for insight. However, another valuable outside source is a close friend. Ask this person to tell you—honestly—what areas of your life you've matured in lately and what areas could still use some work. Together, try to come up with some ideas on how you can strengthen your weak areas, expose any blind spots, and develop any budding talents you may have. Ask your friend to check in on your progress every so often, which will help keep you accountable in following through with your plan.

Each new day is unfamiliar territory. Some of the terrain may look the same, but the truth is, you never know what's beyond the next rise, what new roads and borders God has just ahead for you to cross. The better you know yourself, the better you'll be able to discern the route you need to travel, the road best suited to who you are and who you will yet become.

75
❧
STEP BACK
IN TIME

I t could be a castle on the windswept coast of Scotland. An old plantation home in Georgia. A former concentration camp in Germany. The site of a Catholic mission in California. An Aztec ruin outside of Mexico City. Each place has a story to tell of a specific time in history, of lives that were very different from yours. Yet the people whose feet once walked the same paths you do today also had a lot in common with you. Their hearts resembled your own. They were filled with hopes, fears, and an innate longing to seek the one true God. How did these people respond to these emotions? What joys and difficulties were unique to their own God-chosen times and places in history? What lessons can you learn from their victories and defeats?

Visiting historical sites can be educational. It can give you insight into lessons learned through the years . . . the resilience, ingenuity, and potential depravity of the human spirit. It can help you gain a sense of your own special place in this world. God could have chosen for you to be born anytime, anywhere. Consider both the advantages and challenges you've faced because of the century and geography of your life.

As you step back in time by visiting a site of historical significance, use it to jump-start a few "thank You's" to God. Perhaps you'll want to thank Him for modern conveniences, for the fact that you didn't have to reach your current home by covered wagon, for the privilege of living with religious freedom, or for modern medical advances. Your list can be as unique as you are. Then, ask God to show you what you can apply from the lives of those who have lived before you, from both their mistakes and their sacrifices. Ask God to help you get a clearer picture of the potential your own life story has to benefit future generations.

76

STEP OFF
A CLIFF

I t may seem odd to add "step off a cliff" to your agenda of things to do before you go to heaven. After all, this activity seems more like a way to get to heaven instantly than to help you enjoy life more fully! But when you're outfitted with the right gear—a rock-climbing harness and rappelling rope—stepping off a cliff takes on a whole new dimension. It becomes an adrenaline-pumping life lesson, a visual aid to help you better comprehend what faith really is.

In simple terms, faith is trust. Before you rappel down a vertical wall of rock, you need to trust that the equipment you're using will help you make a safe descent. If you're a first-timer, you need to trust the person who has knotted the rope, helped fasten your harness, and holds your backup "brake" (in case you panic and forget which way is "slow" and which way is "fast" on your rope release!). Even with all these safety precautions in place, leaning back far enough to take that first step off the edge of a cliff is still a tough one. It's a step into unfamiliar territory, a step toward what feels as if you are challenging the law of gravity.

Taking a leap of faith feels the same way. Trusting in a Father you can't reach out and touch is unfamiliar at first. It may feel a little risky, a bit like stepping off into thin air. But trust, or faith, grows when we put it to the test. In the same way that rappelling begins to feel like second nature after you've done it for a while, the more you act on what the Bible says, the easier you'll find it is to trust in the love of that Someone whom you can't see. So, test the sturdy rope of God's words. Rest in the safe harness of His promises. God will never let you down.

77

❧

LOVE AS
IF YOU'LL
NEVER
GET HURT

Love involves risk. It's holding your heart out to others without the assurance that they'll willingly receive it—or return it in one piece. There's also the chance that those you open yourself up to won't open up in return. Despite all of this, God says the most important thing you can do in this life is to love deeply, authentically, and faithfully—the same way He loves you. God asks you to love Him with everything you are and to love others as you love yourself. According to God, extending your love without reservation should be at the top of your list of things to do before you get to heaven.

When you love God wholeheartedly, you never risk rejection. However, you can be certain that loving God will shake up your status quo. It may lead you to cast off some ugly habits, reach out to seemingly unlovable people, and take a giant step out of your comfort zone. But you can love God only to the extent that you know Him. Building a loving relationship with anyone, including God, takes time. Through prayer, reading God's Word, and connecting with others who long to know God the way you do, you'll find that your desire and ability to love and serve God will continue to grow. What's more, your desire and ability to love other fallible humans such as yourself will grow at the same time.

Loving people wholeheartedly does not come with a risk-free guarantee. Every individual comes complete with his or her own unique history, temperament, strengths, weaknesses, and perception of what love really is. That can make loving others tricky at times. The key is to focus on the one thing all people have in common—they are God's irreplaceable children whom He deeply loves. Seeing others through God's eyes, as both valuable and works in progress, will help you reach out without condition and love as if you'll never get hurt.

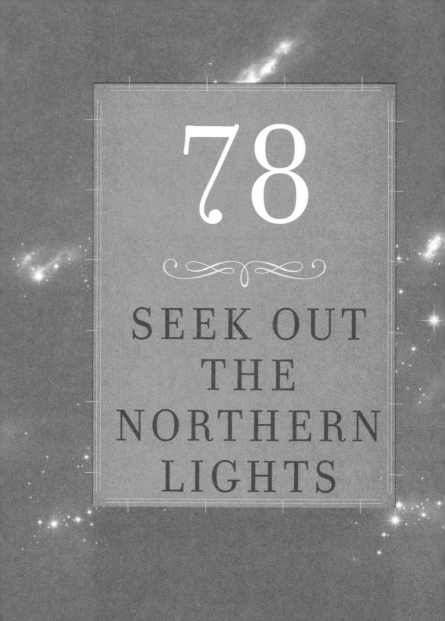

78

SEEK OUT THE NORTHERN LIGHTS

As the sun's solar wind travels through space, it collides with the earth's magnetic field, trapping solar particles that interact with gases from the earth's atmosphere. So? When that happens, the sky comes alive with color as the northern lights come out to play. The scientific phenomenon behind what causes the aurora borealis is of interest to some, but what continues to draw people (including scientists) to look up in awe is its dynamic beauty.

Curtains, swirls, rays, bands, and arcs of green, red, pink, and purple can sweep across the sky. First they move in a stately waltz. Next, a Hungarian polka. Then, as quickly as they appear they vanish, like a smoky mirage in the cold night sky. The color, tempo, and design change from moment to moment and day to day. That means there's no way to guarantee a front-row seat for the performance. You can travel to Northern Canada, Alaska, or Scandinavia during the winter where the aurora is most visible, but then all you can do is watch and wait.

That's part of what makes seeking out the northern lights such a worthy challenge. They paint a perfect picture of waiting on God. As with everything God does, He chooses when the time and conditions are right. All you can do is keep your eyes open for signs of His hand at work. You can't force Him to come when you call. You may even miss seeing His wonders because the storms of life are clouding up your "night sky." That doesn't mean God isn't active, that He isn't making something beautiful right in front of you. Sometimes you may even have to wait until you get to heaven to catch a peek. In the meantime, seek out the northern lights—and remember, God's always at work, coloring your life with the light of His love.

79

PUT YESTERDAY IN ITS PLACE

Life can be lived only one day at a time. All of your yesterdays and tomorrows are out of reach today. But it's tempting to try to drag remnants of your past right along with you all the way into tomorrow—maybe even into heaven itself. The problem is, yesterday is too heavy a load. It has already consumed enough of your time, energy, and emotions the first time around. Why let it steal any of the resources you have at your disposal today?

Put yesterday in its place, behind you where it belongs. If hurts are continuing to make your heart ache, talk to God about them. Picture yourself placing each one of them in His open and able arms so that you're no longer tempted to carry them around with you. Do this every morning, if necessary. If your wounds simply refuse to heal, make an appointment with your pastor or a professional counselor. If there's something you need to make right, do it. Stop putting it off any longer. With God's help, deal with what you've been dealt.

As for the good things that have happened to you in the past, they can hold you back as much as those that have broken your heart. Continuing to hang on to the good old days, to hold tightly to past accolades and accomplishments, to long for the neighborhood, circle of friends, job, or lifestyle you once enjoyed but no longer have, causes only discontentment and distraction. If you're constantly looking back, you're likely to miss the beauty and opportunity God's planted right in front of you. Limit the time and energy you spend on things that are out of your reach—and your control. Allow God to help you be fully present in the present, so you can get the very most out of every day He brings your way.

80

❧ ∞ ❧

REFUSE
TO RETIRE

J ust because you retire from your job doesn't mean you have to retire from life. However, people do it all the time. They believe that as they near the end of their journey toward heaven, their time and their influence on this earth are not as valuable as they were when they were young. So they waste their days. They don't waste them by playing golf, putting together jigsaw puzzles, traveling by motor home, or babysitting the grandkids. Those are great ways to spend a day. They waste them by retreating from life, by refusing to learn new things, meet new people, or continue to grow.

The sad truth is that people can retire from life at twenty-five as easily as they can at sixty-five. Anytime you become more self-focused than God-centered, your growth goes into limbo. Refuse to retire before you get to heaven. Adjust your focus. No matter how old or young you are, God can fill your life with new reasons for joy and use you to make an impact on the world around you.

One way to keep going and growing is to pour yourself into someone else. Become a mentor. Share your woodworking skills with the kid on the corner. Meet with a young mom who could use your years of parenting experience to help her survive her daughter's "terrible twos." Volunteer to be a Big Sister or Big Brother. No matter what stage of life you're in, others could benefit from your experience. Ask God to lead you to someone who needs what you know. Then simply be a friend with a focus. Share what you've learned. Listen as much as you talk. Ask questions. Encourage. Give the one you're mentoring room to grow. Refuse to retire from contributing to God's world as a mentor. You may learn as much as you teach.

81

LEAVE
TRACKS

When a fox is being followed, it will sometimes take a circuitous route, leaving a confusing set of tracks behind in hopes that it will not be found. Like the fox, you are being followed. People who are looking for answers to the biggest questions in life have their eyes on you. Some of these people may be close to your heart. Others you may consider strangers. But they are watching, looking for evidence of someone who really knows God. Someone who knows the way to heaven.

Every day you walk in a way that pleases God, you leave telltale footprints behind. But when the day arrives for you to take the final leg of your journey to heaven, your unique set of tracks on this earth will end. Unlike the fox, you don't want others to "lose your scent." You want to leave behind a set of tracks that are easy to follow, that will lead others straight to the gates of heaven. One simple way to leave tracks that will remain visible, even to future generations, is to make a "homeward bound" box. While a will endows others with your property and possessions, this box can bestow on them the riches of your heart.

Fill it with love. Write letters to friends and family, detailing your hopes and prayers about how God will work in their lives after you are no longer in their presence. Place in it copies of books that God used to change your life. Include a list of favorite Scriptures. Add stories about how you first came to know God and how your relationship with Him changed your life in this world and the next. Every five years or so, review what's in your box. Add, exchange, or delete items as you see fit. Be sure to note in your will where this box can be found, so that after you go to heaven, your tracks will remain, pointing the way to your new home and the One who's waiting there for you.

82

MEMORIZE MORE THAN YOUR TELEPHONE NUMBER

Phone numbers, PIN numbers, Social Security numbers, passwords . . . a lot of odds and ends are filed away in your brain for handy retrieval. Along with personal memories and specific skills you've picked up along the road of life, your brain also retains all the words you know, the names of your friends and relatives, and even the time and day your favorite television show airs. You'd think that after time your brain would reach its limit, but as long as it's functioning properly, it will continue to input information. As a matter of fact, working on your memorization skills can help your brain function at a more effective level.

You could memorize the phone book or the entire script of *Hamlet* to keep your brain in shape, but why not spend your time and energy memorizing something that is good for your heart as well as your brain, something you can use throughout eternity? When you memorize verses from the Bible, God's words are always at hand, whether you are driving a car, facing an unwelcome doctor's visit, or chatting with a friend. Once you've filed them away in your brain, you'll find they pop up when you need them the most.

A few tricks make memorization easier and help you retain longer the information you've memorized. Write down the section of Scripture you want to memorize. Read it aloud five times every morning until you can repeat it by heart. Then, continue to review it at least once a week, until it's totally ingrained in your brain. As research scientists have shown, it's easier to memorize what is meaningful to you. Select verses that you want to keep close to your heart. The more you think about, pray over, and apply the words you are trying to memorize, the more permanent their hold will be on your brain and the greater impact they'll have on your life.

83

WEEP WITH THOSE WHO WEEP

Rejoicing with those who rejoice is fairly easy. You throw a party. You send hearty congratulations. You praise God for what's come about in a friend's life. You join in the fun. However, joining in someone's sorrow is much more difficult.

Just being with a person who is grieving or in physical or emotional pain can feel awkward and uncomfortable. The one you're longing to help may feel angry with God. As a matter of fact, you may too. You struggle to find the right words to say, but there are no words that bring immediate relief. There's nothing you can do to fix things, to make them right. Instead of drying your friend's tears, you're afraid you'll end up adding to them, making things worse instead of better.

The truth is that while rejoicing together can multiply joy, sharing another's sorrow has the power to divide it. To help make another's burden of sorrow lighter, you have to get close enough to that person, and to the pain itself, to be able to reach out and help carry it. The best way to do that is to allow yourself to weep with those who weep. Tears are a prayer without words, a God-given release that acknowledges, "Life is too big to handle on my own." Entering into another's sorrow is a way of joining together in prayer, jointly acknowledging that Earth is not heaven.

God never intended for people to cry alone. He is always close to those whose hearts are broken. He weeps with those who weep. When you do the same, you are following His example. So don't worry about what to say or do. Put yourself in the shoes of the sorrowful. Listen to those who are brokenhearted. Share an embrace. Be attentive to any physical needs you can help fill. And pray, with both words and tears. One day, heaven will dry them all.

84

CREATE A
SIGNATURE
DISH

All of us need a signature dish, a culinary treat we are known for. Think about the people you know who have already established theirs . . . Dad's barbecued ribs, Mom's made-from-scratch chicken potpie, Aunt Maggie's deviled eggs, your best friend's curried chicken salad. If you don't have a signature dish already, it's time to get cooking. And if you do, it's time to get your recipe down pat.

Choose a dish that's just downright delicious. Forget low-cal or low-carb. Select something friends have raved about in the past. It should be unique, but not too exotic. You want something that will please most any palate. It's best to choose a recipe that's fun for you to prepare (even if you make it a lot, which you will) and is easy to whip up without a written recipe. This will come in handy when you're staying at someone's home and want to reciprocate for the hospitality by helping out with the cooking. Keep the ingredients on hand at home so you can pull your specialty together on the spur of the moment. The beauty of having a signature dish is that any-time you're faced with a potluck, unexpected company, or a friend who could use a meal after returning from the hospital, you're pre-pared. You don't need to stress out. You can be generous, sponta-neous, and always ready to spread a little culinary joy.

In the Gospels, Jesus often shared meals with friends. Perhaps His signature dish could be considered fish and bread, which He multiplied miraculously into a more-than-memorable meal for thousands. And with bread and wine, He used food as a visual aid to help others remember Him. Food is a simple, yet significant, part of life here on earth. Use it to make a connection with others, while tantalizing a few taste buds along the way.

85

GO
HUNGRY

When was the last time your stomach growled? When you felt weak because your body lacked nourishment? When you were thankful for one dry crust of bread? When you had no idea where your next meal was coming from? Chances are, these situations are not everyday occurrences in your life. But they are for many people around the globe.

Almost one-half of the world lives on less than two dollars a day. How do two dollars compare with your daily budget? Some people spend more than that on their morning latte fix. This isn't meant to make you feel guilty, just to make you think—and maybe act. Choose to give up food for one day. Drink water, but refrain from eating or drinking anything else. (Check with your doctor to be sure you're healthy enough to do this.) Instead of eating during regular mealtimes, pray for those who spend much of their lives hungry. Let every growl or empty ache in your stomach bring the reality of poverty to your mind and heart. Then, go one step farther. Take the money you would have spent on food that day and send it to a relief organization. Even if it's just a few dollars, you can help nourish a child somewhere around the world or a homeless person in your very own community.

Little sacrifices like this can make a big difference. You may even want to have your family skip one dinner (or simply eat rice and beans as much of the world does) one day a month. Then, donate the money you save. You'll help others, become more aware and empathetic toward those who are less fortunate, more fully appreciate the provisions God's given you, and fulfill the Bible's command to care for the poor. What a great way to spend your time and money!

86

~~~❧~~~

EMBRACE THE PRICKLY PARTS OF LIFE

Living every moment to the fullest sounds like a great philosophy—when life is going well. But who wants to "seize the day" when the day you're supposed to wrap your arms around is as prickly as a desert saguaro? If every day is a gift, some of them seem to be better left unopened. The day you lose your job. The day you get bad news from the doctor's office. The day your fiancé breaks up with you. The day you're in a five-car pileup. The day someone you love departs for heaven, leaving you and your broken heart behind.

The hard truth is that there are going to be painful days on the way to heaven. Whether the pain is emotional, financial, physical, or spiritual doesn't matter. Pain is pain. However, pain can be beneficial—and can even be transformed into something beautiful—if you let it. It all depends on what you choose to do with it.

Instead of fearing it, denying it, getting angry over it, complaining about it, or playing the martyr over it, be brave enough to enter into it. But don't go there alone. God is near. He is compassionate. He is powerful. His arms are big enough to hold both you and your pain long enough, and close enough, not only for you to heal, but to learn lessons that only pain can teach.

Pain forces you to get back to basics. It reminds you about what's really important in life. It helps you appreciate the treasure that an ordinary, uneventful day can hold. It opens your eyes to how God does bring good out of even the most tragic situations. It helps you empathize with others who have walked similar dark roads. And it reminds you that one day the pain of this world will be behind you. Until then, don't waste the pain that comes your way. Learn from it. Embrace it with one hand while holding tightly to God with the other.

87

SPEND
YOURSELF

S ome people live on a constant diet of "someday." Someday they'll lose that ten pounds. Someday they'll start those piano lessons. Someday they'll take that dream trip to the Grand Canyon. Someday they'll get involved at church. Someday they'll get organized, get out of debt, or get that treadmill out of mothballs. Someday they'll be the person God designed them to be. Why save yourself for "someday" when you can spend yourself fully today?

Today can't be saved. It can only be spent. It's a limited-time offer, one-of-a-kind free gift. The same goes for your God-given abilities and opportunities. If you do not use them, you may lose them. The amazing thing is that the opposite is also true. When you put the gifts and talents God has given you into action, you don't use them up; you encourage them to grow. Meanwhile, you unveil an opportunity to glimpse the potential God has placed in you and your unique life.

Although what you do is part of God's potential for your life, who you are is what matters in the end. The real you is revealed and refined by how you choose to spend your days. If you choose to reach out to others in love, to risk failure by putting your abilities to the test, to care for your body in a way that reflects its God-given value, your strengths will rise to the top along with your weaknesses. This will allow you to better see what you need to nurture and what you need God's help to do away with.

Transform your "somedays" into today. Use what God's given you instead of keeping it on a shelf. Ask God to help you spend yourself each day in a way that is true to who you really are—the amazing individual He has designed you to be.

88

TRAVEL OUTSIDE OF YOUR COMFORT ZONE

Think *vacation.* What comes to mind? The chance to sleep in, have fun, get a tan, eat out, catch fish, read a book . . . ? When you have the opportunity to break away from your regular daily schedule, the thought of treating yourself usually rises to the top of your agenda. But at least once before you go to heaven, take a vacation that pushes you outside of your comfort zone instead of setting you squarely in the middle of it. Plan a trip that does more than relax you. Travel somewhere that changes and challenges you.

Give of yourself on vacation instead of expecting others to wait on you. Help build houses in Mexico. Reach out to orphans in the slums of Brazil. Join the Red Cross to aid in an international relief effort. Volunteer to assist a budding church in South Africa. Help provide water for remote villages in the Dominican Republic. Use your career skills to teach dental care to kids in Kenya or English to students in China.

The time you spend helping others is only part of this adventure in vacationing. You'll also be learning lessons that can't be taught in a textbook. You'll learn you can make a friend in a moment. That language barriers can be broken with love. That being challenged can be even more fulfilling than being pampered. That inside, people are all looking for the same thing, regardless of where they live or what language they speak. That simple food can taste like a feast when you're really hungry. That you've been blessed more than you ever realized before.

God has treasures to reveal to you every day of your life, whether you're at work or on vacation. By allowing Him to stretch you in new and different ways, you'll not only become a more flexible person, but a more fulfilled one as well.

89

~∾∾⌇∾∾~

GO BACK
TO SCHOOL

L earning doesn't stop once you're out of school and into adulthood. Learning is a lifelong pursuit. While being an astute student of life is essential as you journey down the road toward heaven, adding an academic endeavor or two along the way can also have benefits. Current research has proven that keeping your brain active can help ward off Alzheimer's disease and dementia, allowing you to use and enjoy every day of your life here on earth to a fuller and more fulfilling degree. Exercising the brain God gave you is as important as exercising your body. Ongoing education is one way of keeping your brain in shape.

Perhaps there's a diploma you regret not having received in the past. Maybe there's a degree you'd like to earn. Or it could be that you saw a flyer in the mail that listed classes at your local community college—and a certain subject caught your eye. The subject you study isn't as important as the passion with which you pursue it. Whether you choose a class to advance your career, complete a degree, learn a specific skill, or simply because it's something you're interested in learning more about, use your time well. Listen. Do the homework. Enter into class discussions. Regardless of your final grade, earn an A for effort, just as you do with the rest of your life.

There is an endless amount of knowledge to be learned in God's universe. What you learn can open the door to opportunities and abilities that may have once been out of your reach. But remember, only God knows it all. And only God can give you the wisdom to use what you know in a way that matters in the scope of eternity. So keep exercising your brain in new ways. Learn new things. Think new thoughts. Stretch your cognitive powers. Then, ask God to help you use what you know in ways that matter. It's the smart thing to do.

90

GREET
THE DAWN

Sunrise comes mighty early. That means you have to get up early to see it. For some people, this is no problem. They are the early birds, the ones who have done a load of wash, sweated through an hour of aerobics, put tonight's dinner in the Crock-Pot, and spent a leisurely time of prayer with God all before most of the rest of humanity has hit the snooze alarm for the first time. The early bird does more than catch the worm. It also gets to witness the dawn of a new day firsthand.

Sunsets are more popular than sunrises, because they happen at a more reasonable hour. But that doesn't make them any less spectacular. Even if you live in an area where the eastern horizon isn't in clear sight, you can still catch the first rays of dawn. The gentle transition from night to light is a treat for the senses, but it's not the only early morning treasure. The hours just after dawn summon those who are awake to bask in the quiet beauty of nature . . . catch sight of dew as it glistens on blades of grass, see flowers stretching to greet the sun by opening the petals they folded shut the night before, hear birds singing before their lilting tunes are drowned out by commuter traffic, wake up to the refreshing nip of crisp morning air. The peace and beauty of early morning seems to invite a time of praise and reflection, as well as a time of preparation for the day ahead.

That doesn't mean you need to greet the dawn every day—unless it's something that fits into your lifestyle. If you are a true night owl, make a point of catching a sunrise every now and then. And when you're on vacation and tempted to sleep in every day, choose one morning to get up early and see the sunrise from a new location. It will help you experience your vacation destination in a whole new light.

91

CONNECT
WITH A
CRITTER

God created all kinds of living things. Some are human. Some come wrapped in fur or scales or ectoskeletons. Not all of them are cuddly or seem to invite relationship. But others immediately do. Dogs, cats, and horses quickly rise to the top of that list. Yet people have been known to become deeply attached to seemingly more standoffish creatures, such as iguanas, pythons, and ferrets. Out of God's whole spectrum of wildlife, at least one species must be calling out to you.

Like everything God has made, animals reveal a bit about the character of their Creator. The sheer number of species speaks of God's creativity, power, and complexity. Their quirky habits and diverse physical forms say something about God's sense of artistry and, perhaps, His sense of humor. The closer you get to animals, the more you understand what miracles they are and the more they can teach you about God and yourself.

This may be nothing new to you. You may have had dogs or cats or fish or birds since you were knee-high to a grasshopper. But if you have never really connected with an animal, never taken the time to care for one, do it before you go to heaven. If you don't want to make the long-term commitment of taking on a pet, offer to pet-sit for a friend. Open yourself up to loving something that can't speak or pay you back for all you've done. Consider what you have in common, and how you differ, from this animal. The longer you spend together, the better chance you'll have of discovering that animals, at least the higher forms, have personalities just as people do. Consider what this says about God—and about the possibility of sharing heaven with some furry friends.

92

SAVE FOR
A SUNNY
DAY

Do something daring. Something unexpected. Something that flies in the face of convention. Refuse to live within your means. Go a step farther: choose to live below your means. It may not be a popular financial plan in these days of credit cards, interest-only mortgages, and a "buy-now-pay-later" mentality. However, it gives you greater freedom to both enjoy and put to use every penny God brings your way.

If you're currently living beyond your means, just learning to live within your means is a worthy goal for the time being. Begin by finding a good financial advisor who can help you get out from under the burden of debt and build a realistic budget. But let your goal be one where saving money is as much of a line item as paying your bills. Each month, put a set percentage of your income into a savings account or easily accessible investment plan. Saving for a rainy day can come in handy when unexpected expenses arise. But don't stop there. Save for sunny days as well.

Set aside a portion of your savings that can provide the means for you to act when God moves you to do something out of the norm . . . Pay the rent for a family struggling with unemployment. Go on a short-term mission trip. Buy a plane ticket for someone who is faced with a family emergency. Buy groceries or school clothes or gasoline or medicine or whatever else someone needs—someone who is facing more rainy days than he or she can count. If you'll invite Him to, God will lead you and act through you to bless others.

When you're experiencing sunny days, being able to help those whose financial picture is currently "all wet" will help you keep things in perspective. Both sunshine and rain are part of God's picture for life here on earth. It helps people learn to lean on one another, and ultimately on Him.

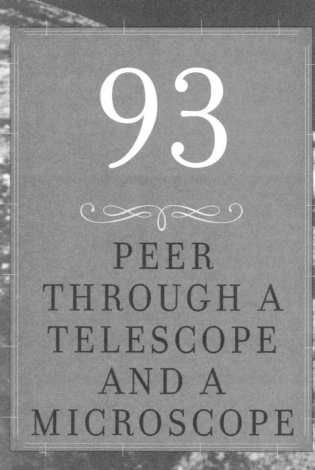

93

PEER
THROUGH A
TELESCOPE
AND A
MICROSCOPE

Think back to your teenage years. Chances are that in high-school science you had the opportunity to look through both a telescope and a microscope. Chances are also pretty good that what you saw was downright astonishing, even if you acted cool and pretended that the rings of Saturn or the minuscule critters swimming in a drop of pond water were nothing special. Before you go to heaven, allow yourself to be astonished all over again.

Visit an observatory or planetarium. Beg or borrow one of those nifty new portable telescopes. Take a trip to a natural history museum or children's science museum. (You may want to take a kid along, if you're still worried about that "cool" thing.) Visit one of those stores at the mall with all the scientific goodies and check out their microscope display. Take advantage of any avenue you can find that will allow you to see what's usually out of your sight, what's hidden from the unaided human eye.

You'll be reminded that there's so much more going on than those things you're aware of each day. A universe of beauty and detail exists both above your head and beneath your feet (not to mention your skin!). The real picture of life in all its intricate order and complexity is so much bigger than what you can see with your eyes. Yet there are limits to what even the most powerful telescope and microscope can reveal.

There is a spiritual universe as complex and ordered as the physical one, one where angels work and God reigns. This universe is as real as the rings of Saturn or the amoebas living in the nearest pond. It simply isn't visible to the human eye. But one day you'll have new eyes that can see the landscape of heaven and the glory of God. Until then, let every telescope and microscope remind you, there's more going on than meets the eye.

94

~~~~~~

TAKE A
STAND

Bumper-sticker philosophy says, "If you don't stand for some-thing, you'll fall for anything." In other words, if your actions don't reflect what you claim you believe, the depth of your beliefs is probably pretty shaky. Your belief in God should be more than a conversation-starter. It should be a life-changer. As your faith deepens and grows, you'll find that what you believe about God will affect every area of your life, including your opinions on social and moral issues. And that belief should move you to act.

You don't have to march on Washington to take a stand for what you believe, although what you believe may compel you to do exactly that. As a matter of fact, what you believe could move you to join your local school board, boycott products that depend on child labor, speak out publicly about stem cell research, campaign for a specific political party . . . and the list goes on and on. It's as varied as the opinions of those who choose to move beyond complaining about what's wrong with the world to actually committing their own time, energy, and resources toward doing something to change it.

Before you go to heaven, choose to stand up for what you feel is important. Make a list of at least five things you believe are worth fighting for. Then, brainstorm about different ways you can support your convictions. Search the Internet for opportunities where you can get involved, or contact a local organization that supports your beliefs in an effective way. Then, put your passion to work. Act on one of the opportunities you find. It may be a one-time commitment, such as working at the polls during the next election. Or it may be an ongoing opportunity, such as helping edit a monthly newsletter that raises funds for and awareness about cancer. Whatever you choose to do, do it in a way that honors God and reflects what you feel matters to Him, as well as to you.

95

❦

SHUN PLANES, TRAINS, AND AUTOMOBILES

Rickshaws, gondolas, ferryboats, chariots, unicycles, dogsleds, covered wagons, hang gliders, paddleboats, snowmobiles, inflatable rafts, kayaks, hot-air balloons . . . even elephants and space shuttles are all modes of transportation. The ways people have found to get from here to there are as varied as the journeys they take. It's true that some methods are more efficient, and comfortable, than others. And if your goal is a speedy trip to the grocery store or your Monday-through-Friday commute to the office, sticking with quick, convenient, and reliable transportation is your best bet.

However, when your time and your budget allow for your journey to be as much of an adventure as the destination is, dare to branch out. Ride a zip line through the canopy of the Costa Rican rain forest. Raft the white water of the Colorado River. Allow a guide to tether you to the steel girders of the Sydney Harbour Bridge. Then walk over the top of the structure, high above the ordinary automobile traffic below. Travel to the floor of the Grand Canyon via donkey. Board a barge for a leisurely cruise through the canals of Belgium. Take a paddle wheeler down the Mississippi. Everywhere you go, keep a lookout for a new way to travel that you may not have tried before.

Every time you board a new mode of transportation, don't simply add it to your "been there, ridden that" list. Begin your journey with prayer. Ask God to help you engage in your adventure fully, experiencing the sights, sounds, smells, bumps, and potholes along the way. Use it as a reminder that the journey of life that God is leading you on is not the fastest way to get you to heaven. But it's the best way to prepare you for the eternal adventure that lies ahead.

96

❦

FIND
BEAUTY IN
BROKEN
THINGS

When something you own breaks, it immediately loses value. It's no longer as useful or beautiful as before. You can try to repair it, but it will never be as good as new. The place where the break originally occurred will usually be more vulnerable to fracturing in the future. Then there's the problem of mended cracks that never totally disappear. They remain visible to the discerning eye, a reminder that what's been broken is no longer whole, no longer perfect. That's why broken things often wind up in the trash. Aren't you glad God doesn't subscribe to that philosophy?

Every person on this earth is broken in one way or another. Relational betrayal, physical ailments, financial difficulties, employment issues, trauma, addiction, abuse . . . a list of the variety of hammers that shatter the human heart is long and brutal. But God promises to bind the wounds of the brokenhearted. Sure, the cracks of your brokenness may still show. You may remain more vulnerable in certain areas of your life. But God will never discard you or consider you less beautiful or valuable because you are not perfect. After all, He's the only One who is.

So, the next time something that's important to you breaks . . . a piece of your grandmother's china crashes to the floor, the spine on your favorite book gives way, a ceramic knickknack (fashioned by pudgy toddler fingers and given to you in honor of Father's Day) is knocked off a shelf . . . do something unexpected. Treasure it, just the way it is. Whether it's in two pieces or twelve, proudly display your broken thing where you can see it every day—where it can remind you of the promises God gives to those who are broken—and the beauty that God finds in every crack in your life that has driven you to reach out to Him.

97

ATTEND
YOUR HIGH-
SCHOOL
REUNION

The next time you find an invitation for a high-school reunion in your mailbox, do something different. Go—as yourself.

Reunions are often like a masquerade ball, with people arriving incognito. They're trying to hide those extra ten pounds, a failed marriage, a career that hasn't lived up to the "most likely to succeed" title they earned way back when. Others are simply trying to hide the hurt, rejection, or loneliness that getting together with the old gang brings back to the surface.

These descriptions may not apply to you. Perhaps high school was your renaissance period and you've been wishing you could turn back the clock since the moment you received your diploma. Perhaps you're living the American dream and can't wait for everyone to notice that your spouse, your job, your house, and your 2.4 kids are proof that you have "arrived." Or maybe, just maybe, you've grown up since your teen years and you're simply looking forward to reconnecting with old friends.

No matter how the person you were in high school compares with the person you are today, risk bringing the two together for one night. It's a great way to evaluate how far you've come and how far you'd still like to go in becoming the person God designed you to be.

But enough about you. After all, that's what adolescence was all about. Now it's time to focus on the rest of your class. After you've caught up with friends you haven't seen in a while, reach out. Talk to the "kids" who were outside your circle of friends. Strike up a conversation with the former "geeks," "jocks," "losers," or "beauty queens" whom you may have labeled instead of really listened to. Listen now. Pray that God will help you see them as He does. Be honest, authentic, and compassionate. You may just make a friend for life.

98

⚜

PONDER A
PANSY

Contemplate a calla lily. Gaze at a gladiola. View a violet. Study a sweet pea. Glimpse a gardenia. Reflect on a rhododendron. Survey a snapdragon. In other words, do more than stop and smell the roses. Take a moment to really look at them. Notice a flower's intricacy and delicacy. Feel its fragile velvet petals. Catch a whiff of its fragrance. Watch how it dances in the breeze.

Every blossom is a creative masterpiece of color and form. Every field of wildflowers is a gallery of glory. Their purpose is simply to be beautiful—and to vividly point out the existence of an intelligent, almighty Creator. Remember, a burning bush on a mountainside is what slowed Moses down long enough to stop and look, so he could hear God's voice. Who's to say that a blazing bougainvillea does not have the power to stop you in your tracks and quiet your heart, so you can hear God speak? Just like Moses, you are on holy ground. God's presence surrounds you. Take off your shoes in awe and wonder.

Make time to look at the miracle of a flower—to notice the extraordinary in the ordinary—as you listen for God's still, small voice. Walk through a neighborhood park or botanical garden. When wildflowers are in bloom, take a hike or a drive, stopping often to look at the complexity of individual blossoms as well as view the broad palette of color that paints the landscape for a brief season. If you have flowers growing in your yard, don't just water and fertilize them. Take a moment to really look at them each day. See how they change. How new buds appear and others fade. Then, take a reminder of God's presence indoors. Keep a vase with a fresh, beautiful blossom in your home throughout the year, a reminder that God cares about the details of your life.

99

RUB SHOULDERS WITH SUFFERING

ince your heart was designed to feel at home in heaven, it's only natural that you will long for earth to feel like your true home. That means your normal human inclination will be to run from suffering and protect yourself from pain. However, if you look at Jesus' life, He did just the opposite. Here's an opportunity to follow in His footsteps.

Since no tears or pain will be in heaven, your time here on earth offers your only chance to rub shoulders with suffering. You may feel as though you have all the suffering you can handle in your own life. Or, if you feel things are going well, you may wonder why you'd want to mess with allowing someone else's pain to pollute your peace. The truth is that a miracle happens when you enter into someone else's suffering. You become God's hands and feet. You become a tangible expression of an invisible God. The comfort, encouragement, and hope you offer flows straight from heaven's throne. You bring a bit of heaven down to earth.

Where to begin is up to you. Just open your eyes and your heart. Then put your compassion into action. Take hot coffee to the homeless when the winter winds begin to blow. Go on a mission trip to a third-world country. Work at a soup kitchen or homeless shelter. Listen to and pray with a friend who's grieving. Adopt a grandparent at a rest home. Volunteer at a hospital or prison ministry. It won't be easy. You can't expect to snuggle up to suffering and come away untouched. Your heart may ache. People may be ungrateful. But never doubt that what you do makes a difference. God's hands and feet always leave an eternal imprint of love.

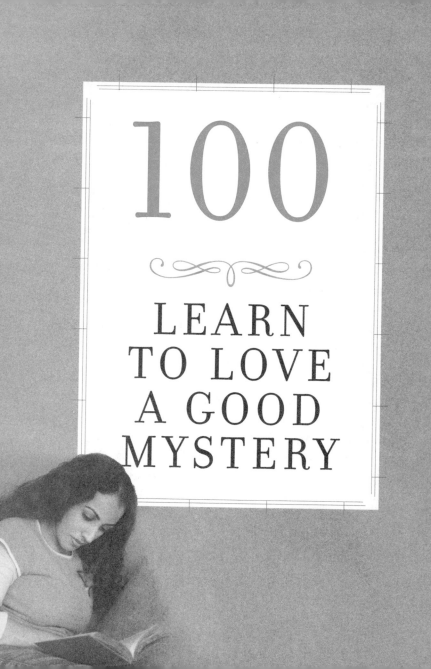

100

LEARN TO LOVE A GOOD MYSTERY

A good mystery captures your imagination and holds your attention, right up to the point where it's finally solved. In the thick of the story, many of the clues seem disjointed, so much so that some of the story's sidelines may not seem important at all. But once all of the clues fall into place, there's an "aha" moment. Finally, everything makes sense.

Life is not just a good mystery, it's a great one. You already know "whodunit" and that the motive is love. Knowing that God is both the main character and the Author of the mystery also helps you put a few of the seemingly unconnected clues together. It helps you make some sense out of life. But you can read the final chapter only in heaven. In His wisdom, God doesn't allow you to skip ahead, have the ending all figured out, and then go back and get acquainted with the middle of the story. If He did, you'd miss out on some of the excitement, beauty, and wonder along the way. You'd miss out on the pull of the mystery.

But living in the midst of a mystery can get frustrating at times. So many questions have not yet been fully answered—questions about things such as suffering and justice and salvation and prayer. To be able to focus on the chapter you're living right now means having to live with some unanswered questions. It means learning to trust the Author enough to know that not only will He tie everything together in the end, but He will weave you into a wonderful, engaging story on the way there. So pay attention to the details. Look for clues along the way. Live every page to the fullest. This is a mystery that will be written, and lived, only once in an eternity.

101

DO WHAT'S LAST ON YOUR LIST

If today were the day you were heading to heaven, is there anything you'd regret not having done before you leave this earth? Take a moment to look around at those whose lives have crossed yours over the course of your lifetime. Is there anyone you cannot look in the eye? It could be a friend, a relative, even God Himself. You know in your gut that there's something you should do. Maybe you need to extend a heartfelt apology. Be more vocal about your love. Offer forgiveness. Repay a long-neglected debt. Or maybe what you need to do most is wholly give your heart to the One who's prepared a special place in heaven just for you.

If you have not yet embarked on a personal relationship with God through His Son, Jesus Christ, then this is your moment—the most significant moment of your life, both earthly and eternal. Don't let it pass without reaching out and taking the hand of the Savior. He's given His all for you. He stepped down from His throne, left the glorious perimeters of heaven and allowed Himself to be born as a human being, so that He could take upon Himself the entire responsibility for every unholy and unrighteous thought you've ever thought, deed you've ever done, word you've ever spoken. Then He carried it all with Him to the Cross, where He received the punishment due the worst of criminals and paid the ultimate price for your sins.

Now Jesus longs to bring you to the Father, to introduce you to His love and His grace, to help you become all He created you to be. The Bible says He stands at the door of your heart and knocks. Won't you open the door and ask Him to come in allowing Him to be your Savior and the Lord of your life? The decision is yours—but don't hesitate. Heaven waits!

NOW IT'S YOUR TURN.
BEFORE GOING TO HEAVEN,
I'D LIKE TO . . .

_____

_____

_____

_____

_____

_____

_____

_____

_____

_____

_____

_____

_____

_____

_____

_____

THOUGHTS OF JOY FOR LIFE'S JOURNEY

I believe in life after birth.

MAXIE DUNHAM
THOUGHTS FOR THE JOURNEY

We live but a fraction of our life. Why do we not let in the flood,
raise the gates, and set all our wheels in motion? He that hath ears to
hear, let him hear. Employ your senses.

HENRY DAVID THOREAU
JOURNAL

Seize from every moment its unique novelty,
and do not prepare your joys.

ANDRÉ GIDE

Life is a romantic business. It is painting a picture, not doing a sum—
but you have to make the romance, and it will come to the question
how much fire you have in your belly.

JUSTICE OLIVER WENDELL HOLMES

BEFORE GOING TO HEAVEN, I'D LIKE TO . . .

THOUGHTS OF JOY FOR LIFE'S JOURNEY

Pursue, keep up with, circle round and round your life,
as a dog does his master's chaise. Do what you love.
Know your own bone; gnaw at it, bury it, unearth it,
and gnaw it still.
HENRY DAVID THOREAU

I simply believe that there is a mystery of the ordinary,
that the commonplace is full of wonder, and that this life
that we call Christian is different from what we think it is.
It is infinitely more subtle, more powerful, more dangerous,
more magnificent, more exciting, more humorous, more delicious,
more adventurous, more involved, and more troublesome
than most of us think.
TIM HANSEL

BEFORE GOING TO HEAVEN, I'D LIKE TO . . .

THOUGHTS OF JOY FOR LIFE'S JOURNEY

It costs so much to be a full human being that there are very few who
have the enlightenment, or the courage, to pay the price. . . .
One has to abandon altogether the search for security,
and reach out to the risk of living with both arms.
One has to embrace the world like a lover, and yet demand no easy
return of love. One has to accept pain as a condition of existence.
One has to court doubt and darkness as the cost of knowing.
One needs a will stubborn in conflict, but apt always to the total
acceptance of every consequence of living and dying.

MORRIS L. WEST
THE SHOES OF THE FISHERMAN

Living is
a thing you do
now or never—
which do you?

PIET HEIN
LIVING IS—

BEFORE GOING TO HEAVEN, I'D LIKE TO . . .

_____

_____

_____

_____

_____

_____

_____

_____

_____

_____

_____

_____

_____

_____

_____

_____

_____

THOUGHTS OF JOY FOR LIFE'S JOURNEY

Listen to the Exhortation of the Dawn!
Look to this Day!
For it is Life, the very Life of Life.
In its brief course lie all the
Verities and Realities of your Existence.
The Bliss of Growth,
The Glory of Action,
The Splendor of Beauty;
For Yesterday is but a Dream,
And Tomorrow is only a Vision:
But Today well liked makes
Every Yesterday a Dream of Happiness,
And every Tomorrow a Vision of Hope.
Look well therefore to this Day!
Such is the Salutation of the Dawn!

AUTHOR UNKNOWN
TAKEN FROM THE SANSKRIT AND ATTRIBUTED BY SOME SOURCES TO
A FIFTH–CENTURY DRAMATIST AND LYRIC POET

BEFORE GOING TO HEAVEN, I'D LIKE TO . . .

THOUGHTS OF JOY FOR LIFE'S JOURNEY

Our Father refreshes us on the journey
with some pleasant inns but will not encourage us
to mistake them for home.

C. S. LEWIS

You [God] have made known to me the paths of life;
you will fill me with joy in your presence.

ACTS 2:28